HARCOURT
Science
CALIFORNIA EDITION

Harcourt School Publishers

Orlando • Boston • Dallas • Chicago • San Diego

www.harcourtschool.com

Cover Image
This is a Bengal tiger cub. The Bengal tiger is a native of India and is an endangered animal.

ISBN 0-15-317651-2

5 6 7 8 9 10 032 2002 2001

Authors

Marjorie Slavick Frank
Former Adjunct Faculty Member at
 Hunter, Brooklyn, and Manhattan
 Colleges
New York, New York

Robert M. Jones
Professor of Education
University of Houston-Clear Lake
Houston, Texas

Gerald H. Krockover
Professor of Earth and Atmospheric
 Science Education
School Mathematics and Science
 Center
Purdue University
West Lafayette, Indiana

Mozell P. Lang
Science Education Consultant
Michigan Department of Education
Lansing, Michigan

Joyce C. McLeod
Visiting Professor
Rollins College
Winter Park, Florida

Carol J. Valenta
Vice President—Education,
 Exhibits, and Programs
St. Louis Science Center
St. Louis, Missouri
Former teacher, principal, and
 Coordinator of Science Center
 Instructional Programs
Los Angeles Unified School District
Los Angeles, California

Barry A. Van Deman
Science Program Director
Arlington, Virginia

Senior Editorial Advisor

Napoleon Adebola Bryant, Jr.
Professor Emeritus of Education
Xavier University
Cincinnati, Ohio

Program Advisors

Michael J. Bell
Assistant Professor of Early
 Childhood Education
School of Education
University of Houston-Clear Lake
Houston, Texas

George W. Bright
Professor of Mathematics Education
The University of North Carolina at
 Greensboro
Greensboro, North Carolina

Pansy Cowder
Science Specialist
Tampa, Florida

Robert H. Fronk
Head, Science/Mathematics
 Education Department
Florida Institute of Technology
Melbourne, Florida

Gloria R. Guerrero
Education Consultant
Specialist in English as a Second
 Language
San Antonio, Texas

Bernard A. Harris, Jr.
Physician and Former Astronaut
*(STS 55—Space Shuttle Columbia,
STS 63—Space Shuttle Discovery)*
Vice President, SPACEHAB Inc.
Houston, Texas

Lois Harrison-Jones
Education and Management
 Consultant
Dallas, Texas

Linda Levine
Educational Consultant
Orlando, Florida

Kenneth R. Mechling
Professor of Biology and Science
 Education
Clarion University of Pennsylvania
Clarion, Pennsylvania

Barbara ten Brink
Science Director
Round Rock Independent School
 District
Round Rock, Texas

Reviewers and Contributors

Gwendolyn C. Manning
Teacher, Gibsonville Elementary
Gibsonville, North Carolina

Deborah Moilanen
Curriculum, Grade Level Specialist
Plano ISD
Plano, Texas

Michael F. Ryan
Educational Technology Specialist
Lake County Schools
Tavares, Florida

Kathleen Schaeffer
Teacher, Hawthorne School
Beverly Hills, California

Judy Taylor
Teacher, Silvestri Junior High School
Las Vegas, Nevada

★3

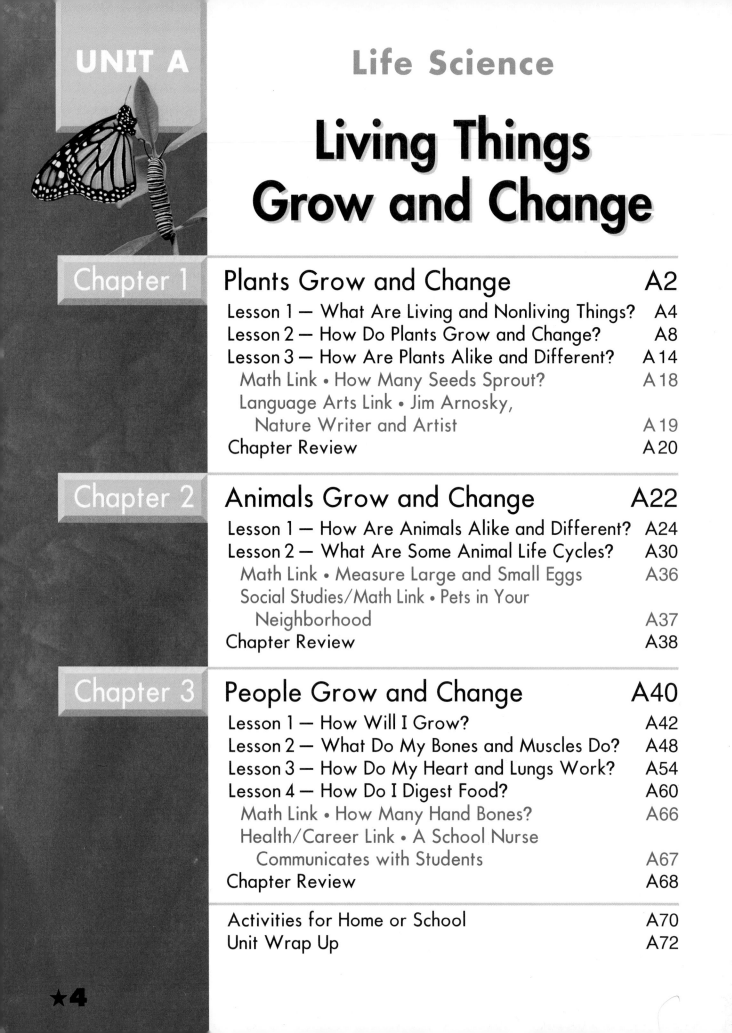

UNIT A

Life Science

Living Things Grow and Change

Earth Science

Exploring Earth's Surface

Physical Science

Matter and Motion

Extension Chapters

Introduction and References

Using Science Skills

Observe.

Use your five senses to help you learn.

Compare.

Tell how things are alike and different.

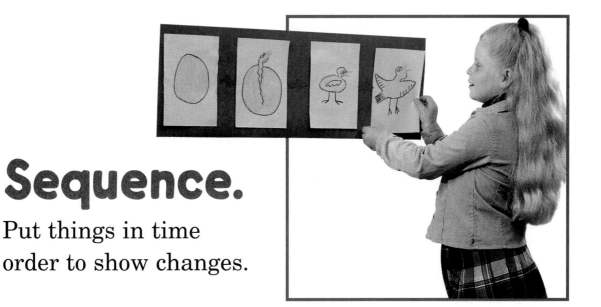

Sequence.

Put things in time order to show changes.

Classify.

Sort objects into groups to show how they are alike.

Infer.

Use what you know to make a good guess about why something is happening.

Gather information.

Use computers, books, and what you observe.

Plan.

Decide step by step how to investigate your ideas.

Make models.

Make something to show what a thing is like or how it works.

Measure.

Use tools to find out how far or how much.

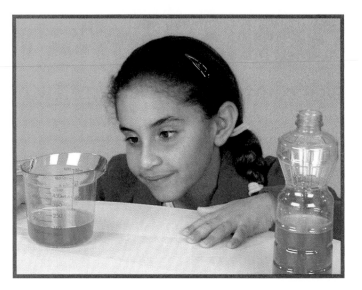

Predict.

Use what you know to make a good guess about what will happen.

Draw conclusions.

Use all the information you have gathered to make decisions.

Communicate.

Share what you know by telling or showing others.

Science Safety

Think ahead.

Be neat.

Be careful.

Do not eat or drink things.

Safety Symbols

CAUTION Be careful!

CAUTION Sharp!

CAUTION Be careful!

CAUTION Wear an apron.

CAUTION Wear goggles.

Living Things
Grow and Change

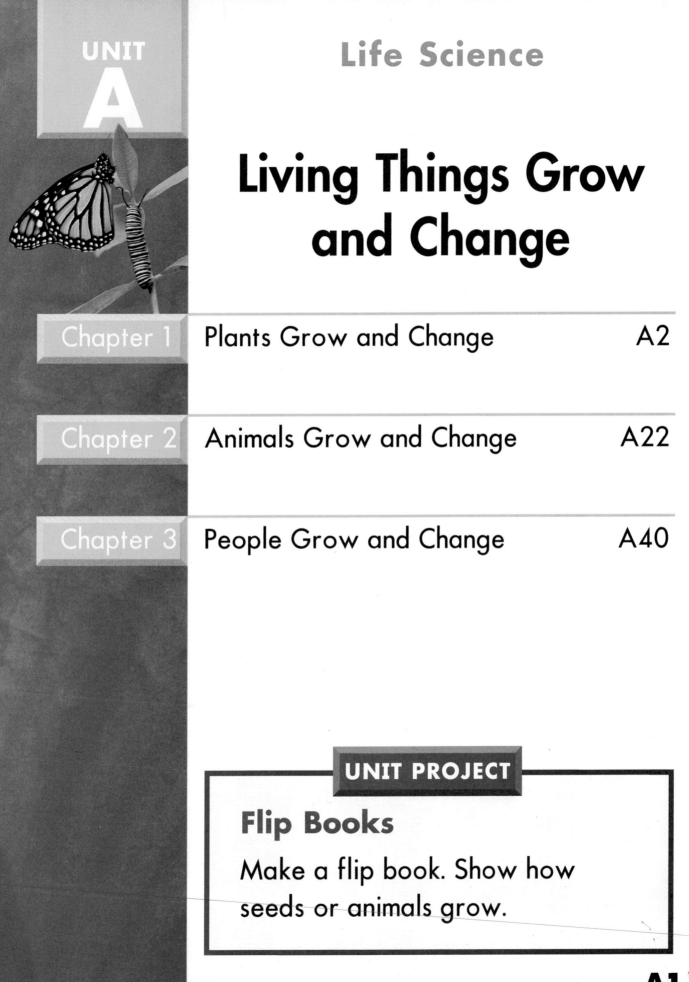

UNIT

A

Life Science

Living Things Grow and Change

UNIT PROJECT

Flip Books

Make a flip book. Show how seeds or animals grow.

A1

Plants Grow and Change

Vocabulary

living
nonliving
nutrients
seed coat
germinate
seedling
cactus

Did You Know?
The redwood tree is the tallest **living** thing in the United States.

Did You Know?

The part of popcorn that sticks between your teeth is the **seed coat**.

What Are Living and Nonliving Things?

Living and Nonliving Things

You will need

picture cards

paper and pencil

What Am I?	
Living	Nonliving

1 Make a chart like the one above.

2 Look at each picture card. Does it show a living thing or a nonliving thing?

3 Record in your chart.

4 Compare the things in the chart.

Science Skill

When you compare things, you tell how they are alike and different.

Living and Nonliving Things

The world is made up of living things and nonliving things. All **living** things grow and change. They need food, water, and air. Things that are not alive are **nonliving**. They do not need food, water, and air.

nonliving things

living things

Living Things Grow and Change

A tree and a chick are living things. They come from other living things. Like all living things, they need food, air, and water. Like all living things, they grow and change.

■ **How do you think the chick will change?**

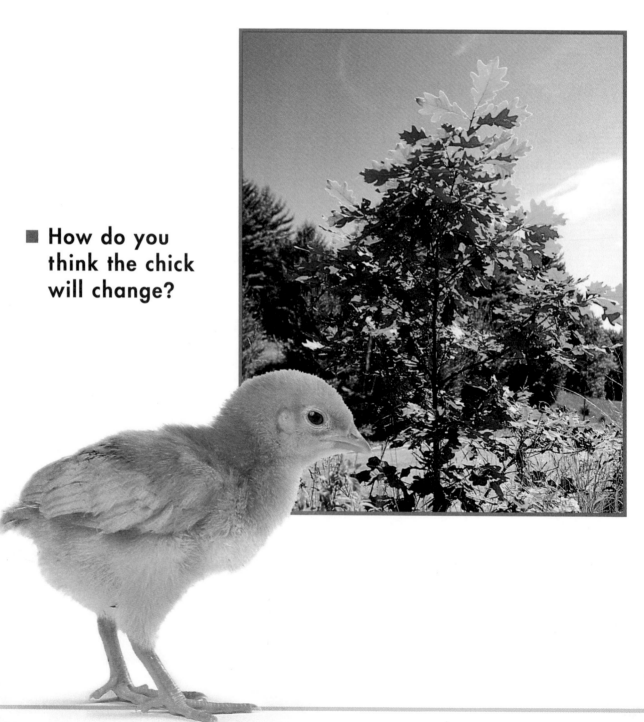

Environment Affects Living Things

A living thing's environment, or what is around it, affects what the living thing looks like and how it grows. A plant that does not get enough light and air will not be healthy.

The amount of food an adult male deer eats affects the size of his <u>antlers</u>. One that eats more food will have larger antlers than one that does not get enough food.

■ **Which of these deer probably eats more food?**

Think About It

1. What are three ways living things are alike?
2. What affects the way living things look and grow?

How Do Plants Grow and Change?

Investigate

What Plants Need

You will need

2 plants

cup of water

paper and pencil

What Happens to a Plant	
Plant with Water	Plant with No Water

1. Make a chart like the one above.

2. Put both plants in a sunny place. Water the soil of only one plant. Predict what will happen.

3. Observe both plants every day. Write the date. Record any changes.

Science Skill

When you observe the plants, use your senses of sight, touch, smell, and hearing.

What the Parts of a Plant Do

A plant needs light, air, and water to grow. It also needs **nutrients**, or minerals, from soil. Each part of a plant helps the plant get what it needs. When a plant gets what it needs, it can grow and change.

Flowers make seeds that can grow into new plants.

Leaves use light, air, water, and nutrients to make food for the plant.

Stems hold up the plant and move water and nutrients through it.

Roots take in water and nutrients from the soil.

How Plants Grow from Seeds

Seeds have different parts. Most seeds have a covering called a **seed coat**, which protects the seed. The seed is made up of stored food and a tiny plant. The tiny plant uses the stored food when it begins to grow.

When a seed gets water and warmth, it may **germinate**, or start to grow. First the roots grow down. Then a stem grows up. The young plant is called a **seedling**.

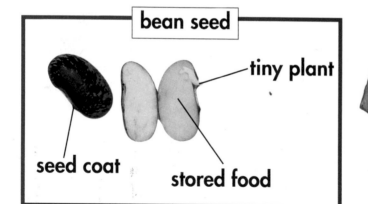

bean seed

tiny plant

seed coat

stored food

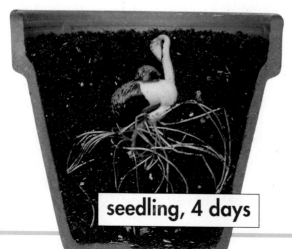

seedling, 4 days

seedling, 15 days

As the seedling grows, it makes more leaves and stems. The stems get taller and thicker. When the plant is full grown, seeds form in one part of each flower. This flower part becomes a fruit that protects the seeds. The seeds may later germinate and grow into a new plant.

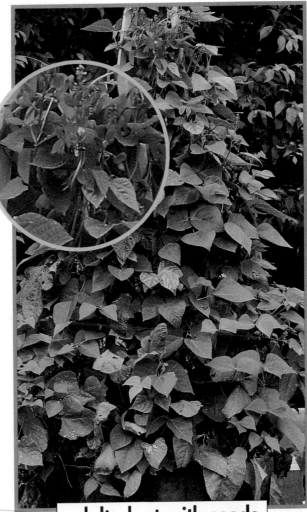

adult plant with seeds

plant, 45 days

Plants Can Change

If plants do not get what they need, they may not grow. The rain, sunlight, and even insects in a place can make the plants change. If a field does not get rain for a long time, the plants there will not get the water they need.

■ How can you tell that these plants did not get the water they needed?

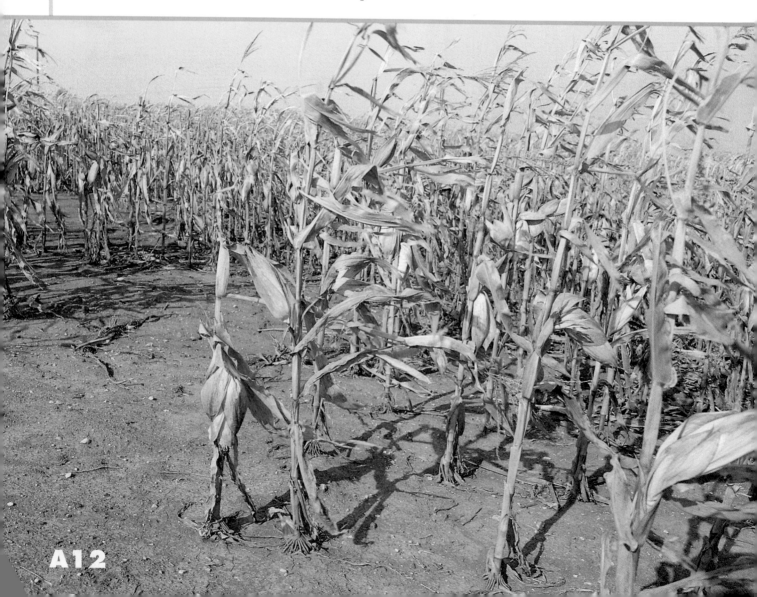

A plant needs light from all sides. If it gets light from just one side, its stems and leaves grow toward the light. This helps the plant get the light it needs to make food and grow.

■ **Why does this plant grow toward the light?**

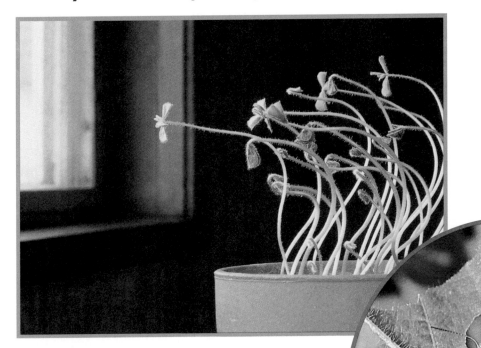

Insects may eat the leaves of a plant. Without leaves, the plant cannot make the food it needs. It may die.

Think About It

1. What happens when a seed germinates?
2. What are some ways plants may change?

How Are Plants Alike and Different?

Investigate

How to Classify Leaves

You will need

leaves

index cards and pencil

1 Observe the leaves. Look for ways they are alike.

2 Classify the leaves into groups. Leaves in each group should be alike in some way.

3 Write a label for each group that tells how the leaves are alike. Tell classmates about the leaves where you live.

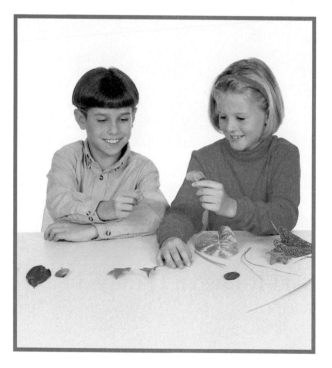

Science Skill
When you classify things, you sort them into groups that show how they are alike.

Plants in Different Places

Plants live in almost every part of the world. Different kinds of plants grow in different places.

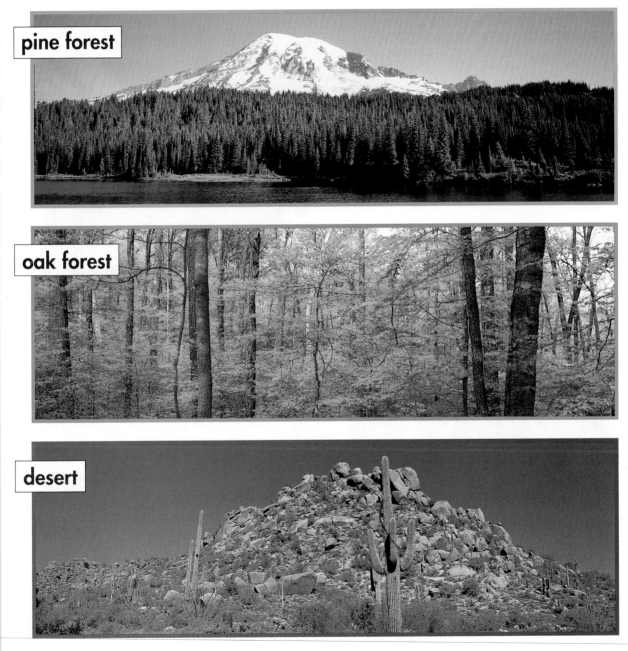

pine forest

oak forest

desert

How Plants Are Different

A pine tree has leaves that look like needles. Its small, hard seeds grow in cones. The outside of the cone protects the seeds until they are ready to germinate.

An oak tree has leaves that are broad and flat. Oak trees grow from seeds called acorns.

pine cone

pine seeds

acorns

■ How is an acorn different from a pine cone?

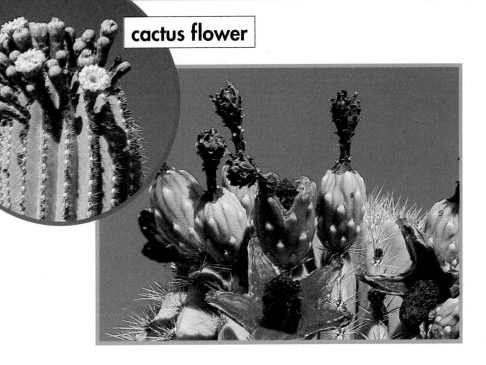

cactus flower

A **cactus** plant can store water in its thick stems. Its leaves are sharp spines. The spines protect the stems from animals that might eat them.

Cactuses also grow flowers. Like all flowers, cactus flowers grow into fruits. The cactus seeds are inside the fruits.

Think About It

1. What are some places plants live?
2. How are plants in different places alike and different?

A17

Math Link

How Many Seeds Sprout?

Hundreds of walnuts grow on this walnut tree. A new tree could grow from each walnut. Most of the walnuts will not germinate. Animals will eat some of them. Others will not get the things they need to grow.

Think and Do

Count and record the number of seeds in an orange. Then plant the seeds. Make sure they have water and warmth. Count and record the number of seeds that germinate and grow. Write a subtraction sentence that tells how many seeds did not grow.

Jim Arnosky, Nature Writer and Artist

Jim Arnosky first worked as a naturalist. A naturalist studies plants and animals in the wild. Now Jim Arnosky writes and illustrates children's books. In some of his books, the character Crinkleroot helps children learn about living things in nature.

Think and Do

Draw your own character. Use your character in a story about living things. Share your story.

A19

Tell What You Know

1. How are these plants alike and different?

2. How did these plants grow from seeds?

3. How does the environment affect these plants?

Vocabulary

Tell the term that completes the sentence.

seedling   **germinate**   **nutrients**
        living thing   **nonliving thing**

4. Plants need water and warmth to _____ .

5. A _____ does not need food, water, and air.

6. A _____ is a young plant.

7. Plants need _____ , or minerals, from the soil.

8. A _____ grows and changes.

A20

Using Science Skills

9. Observe and Compare Make a chart like this one to record what you observe about seeds. Tape seeds from different plants onto the chart. Tell what plant each seed comes from. Write your observations in the chart. Compare your observations with those of a classmate.

What I Observe About Seeds		
Seed	Plant	Observations

10. Classify Sort things in your classroom into groups of living things and nonliving things. List the things in each group. Tell why you put each thing in the group you did.

Animals Grow and Change

Vocabulary

mammal
reptile
amphibian
insect
life cycle

Did You Know?
The largest **mammal** in the world is the blue whale.

Did You Know?
The walking stick is the longest **insect** in the world. It is 13 inches long.

How Are Animals Alike and Different?

Ways to Group Animals

You will need

animal picture cards

index cards and pencil

1 Observe the animals to see how they are alike and different.

2 Classify the animals into groups. Animals in a group should be alike somehow.

3 Write a label for each group that tells how the animals are alike.

Science Skill

When you classify animals, you put them into groups to show how the animals are alike.

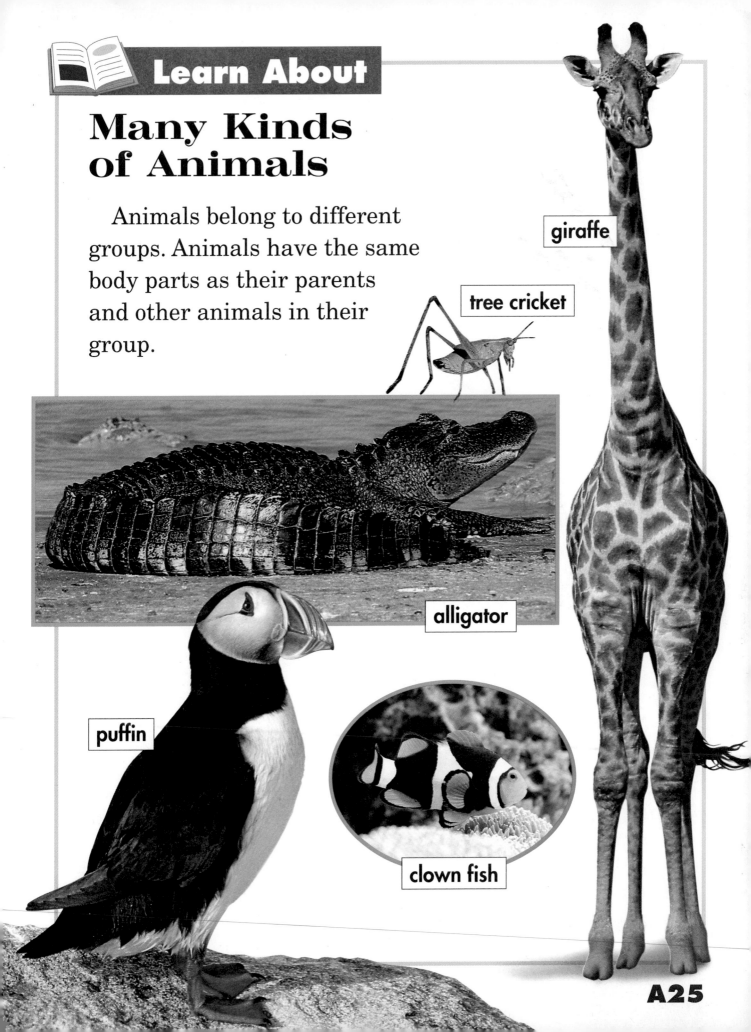

Learn About

Many Kinds of Animals

Animals belong to different groups. Animals have the same body parts as their parents and other animals in their group.

giraffe

tree cricket

alligator

puffin

clown fish

Animals With Bones

Animals can be grouped by their body parts. All the animals on these two pages have bones inside their bodies. They have other body parts that make them different.

Cats and dogs are mammals. A **mammal** is an animal that has fur or hair. A mother mammal makes milk and feeds it to her young.

Birds have feathers to protect their bodies. They also have wings. Most birds use their wings to fly.

blue jay

chameleon

Lizards, snakes, and turtles are reptiles. A **reptile** is an animal that is covered with scales. Its skin is rough and dry.

Frogs and toads are amphibians. An **amphibian** often has smooth, wet skin. Its skin helps it live both in water and on land.

All fish live in water. A fish uses its fins to swim and its gills to breathe.

■ **What tells you that these animals are not mammals?**

leaf frog

fish

Animals Without Bones

The animals on these two pages have no bones. They have other body parts that make them different.

Praying mantises, ants, and bees are insects. An **insect** is an animal that has three body parts and six legs. Many insects also have four wings. Spiders are not insects. They have eight legs.

praying mantis

golden silk spider

Worms have soft bodies. They do not use legs to walk. Instead, worms use their bodies to crawl.

Like a worm, a snail has a soft body that it uses to move. It may also have a hard shell to protect it.

snail

earthworm

■ **How are the worm and the snail alike and different?**

Think About It

1. What are some ways animals are alike? How are they different?
2. How can animals be grouped by their body parts?

What Are Some Animal Life Cycles?

Investigate

How Mealworms Grow and Change

You will need

mealworms

mealworm home with meal

bottle cap with water

hand lens

1 Place the mealworms in the meal. Give them water each day.

2 Observe the mealworms every day with the hand lens.

3 Each day draw a picture of what you observe. Write the date and a sentence about changes you see.

Science Skill

You can use a hand lens to help you observe details.

How Animals Grow and Change

These goslings and the lion cub are still young. They will keep growing and changing. They will grow up to look like their parents. Together, all the parts of an animal's life from birth to death make up its **life cycle**.

Canada geese

goslings

African lions

cub

How Birds Grow and Change

Birds lay eggs. First, a mother bird lays her eggs in a nest. Next, the mother or father sits on the eggs to keep them warm.

A chick grows inside each egg until it gets too big for it. Then the chick breaks the eggshell and hatches.

As the chicks grow and change, they get new feathers. They will grow up to look like their parents.

unhatched eggs in nest

Life Cycle of a Robin

adult bird

Most bird parents take care of their chicks. The parents feed and protect them until they can take care of themselves. Soon after the birds are grown, they can have chicks of their own.

chick just hatched

chick almost ready to fly

How Mammals Grow and Change

All young mammals start growing inside their mothers' bodies. The adult cat here has kittens growing inside her. When they are big enough, the kittens will be born. They will grow up and have features like their parents.

Life Cycle of a Cat

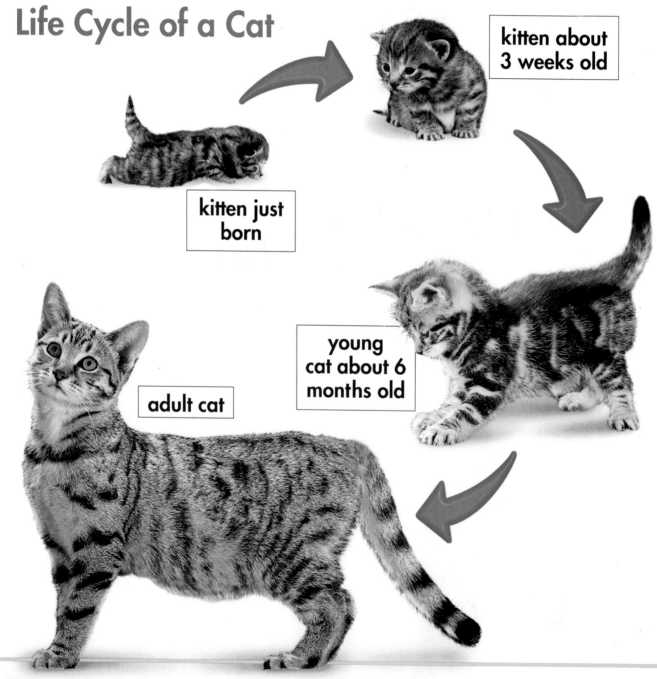

kitten about 3 weeks old

kitten just born

young cat about 6 months old

adult cat

Like all young mammals, these kittens drink milk from their mother. The milk helps the kittens grow bigger and stronger. By the time they are one year old, they are full grown.

■ Kittens may not look exactly like either parent. A kitten gets some of its features from its mother and some from its father.

Think About It

1. What do young animals grow to look like?
2. How might an animal be different from other animals of its own kind?

Differences in Animals of the Same Kind

Animals of the same kind are not all exactly alike. Some are larger or stronger. They have different markings. How do these wolves look different from one another?

timberwolves

Math Link

Measure Large and Small Eggs

The ostrich lays the biggest eggs. The hummingbird lays the smallest eggs. Compare the sizes of the eggs to the size of a chicken egg.

ostrich egg

chicken egg

hummingbird egg

Think and Do

The photographs show the real sizes of eggs from different birds. Use a ruler to measure the picture of each egg. Make a chart and list the kinds of eggs in order from biggest to smallest. Beside each name, write how long the egg is.

Social Studies/Math Link

Pets in Your Neighborhood

People keep many kinds of animals as pets. In many neighborhoods, people have dogs and cats. Dogs and cats are mammals. Some people have reptiles, fish, and birds.

Think and Do

Talk to classmates or neighbors who have pets. Think about the animal group each pet belongs to. Show what you find out in a bar graph. Use the graph to talk about which animal groups most of the pets belong to.

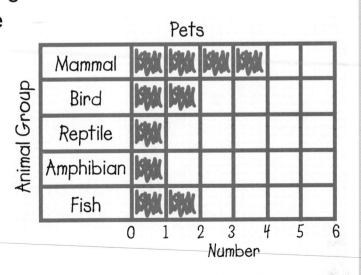

Pets

Animal Group	Number					
	0	1	2	3	4	5	6
Mammal	▨	▨	▨	▨			
Bird	▨	▨					
Reptile	▨						
Amphibian	▨						
Fish	▨	▨					

A37

Tell What You Know

1. How are these animals alike?
2. How are the animals different?
3. What is the life cycle of each animal?

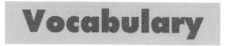
Vocabulary

Tell the term that completes the sentence.

amphibian	reptile	mammal
insect	life cycle	

4. An _____ has six legs.

5. A _____ has scales that are rough and dry.

6. A _____ has fur or hair.

7. A _____ is the way an animal grows and changes.

8. An _____ has smooth, wet skin.

Using Science Skills

9. **Classify** Go for a walk outside with your class. Look for different kinds of animals. Write down the name of each one you see. What animal group does it belong to? Write the group name next to the animal name.

   Then think about whether you saw two animals of the same kind. If you did, tell how they looked different from each other.

Animal	Kind
robin	bird
squirrel	mammal
bee	insect

10. **Observe** These pictures show the life cycle of a butterfly. Observe the changes from one picture to the next. Think about what you know about animal life cycles. Then use the pictures to tell what happens in a butterfly's life cycle.

People Grow and Change

Vocabulary

permanent teeth

skeleton

muscles

heart

lungs

heart rate

digest

saliva

stomach

Did You Know?
Your **heart** beats more than 66 times a minute.

Did You Know?
It takes 43 **muscles** to frown but only 17 muscles to smile.

How Will I Grow?

How Hands Grow and Change

You will need

paper and pencil

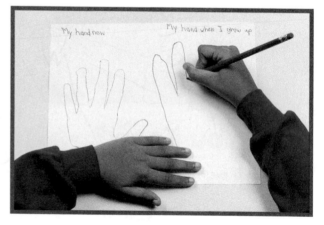

1 Trace your hand on the left side of your paper.

2 Predict what your hand will look like when you grow up. Draw a picture of it.

3 Compare the two hands. Tell how they are alike and different.

Science Skill

When you predict, you use what you know to make a good guess about what will happen.

How Your Body Grows and Changes

Your body grows and changes in many ways. You get bigger and taller. You get stronger and heavier. How has the boy in these pictures grown and changed?

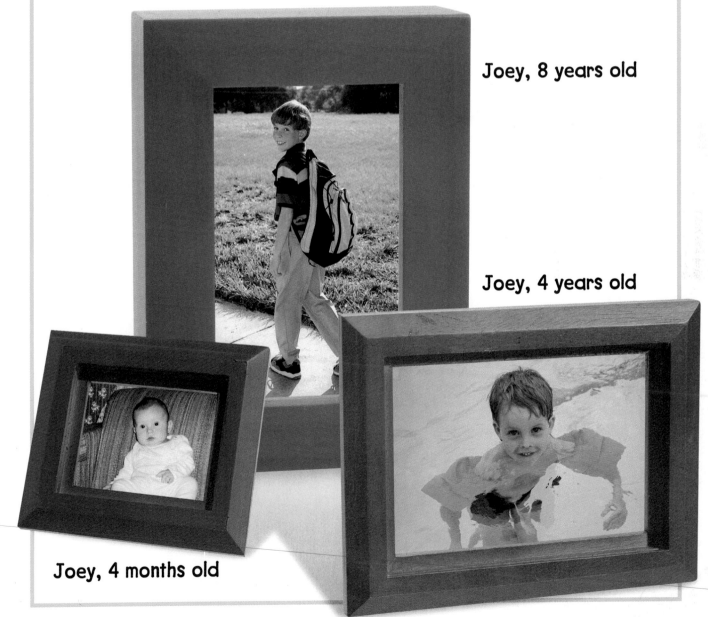

Joey, 8 years old

Joey, 4 years old

Joey, 4 months old

A43

All People Grow and Change

No two people are exactly alike, but all people grow and change. You are growing and changing. First, you were a baby. Now, you are a child. Later on, you will be a teenager. After that, you will become an adult like your parents.

■ **Predict how the three children in this family will grow and change.**

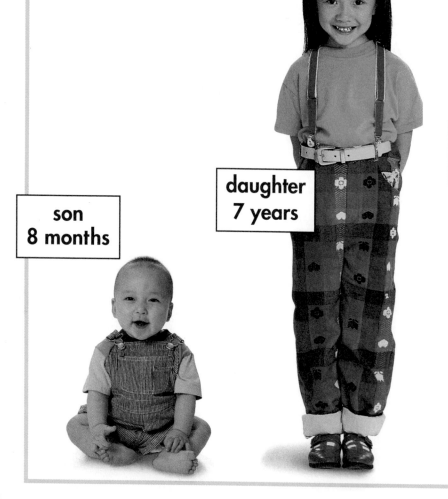

son
8 months

daughter
7 years

son
15 years

When you are an adult, you will change in other ways. As you get older, your hair may turn gray or white. Your skin will get wrinkles.

mother
37 years

father
42 years

grandmother
65 years

Growing in Other Ways

Growing is more than getting bigger. You also change in other ways as you grow. When you were a baby, your first teeth grew in. Now you are losing those teeth. New adult teeth, called **permanent teeth**, are growing in to take their place.

Learning is another way you grow and change. You are changing as you learn new things.

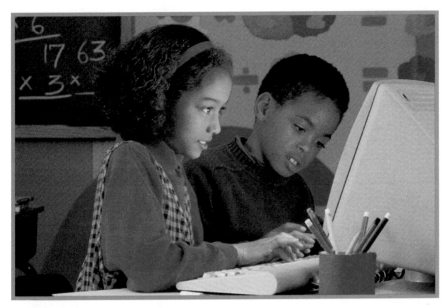

Some things you learn can also help you exercise. Exercise such as dancing helps your body grow strong and stay healthy.

- **How is this girl helping her body? What is she learning?**

Think About It

1. How do people grow and change?
2. How can you help yourself grow and change?

What Do My Bones and Muscles Do?

How Your Elbow Works

You will need

balloon

tape

3 rubber bands

2 paper towel tubes, each with a hole

1. Make a model elbow. Tie the tube ends together with a rubber band. Tape the rubber band in place.

2. Attach each end of the balloon to a tube, as you see here.

3. Open and close the tubes. Tell how this model is like your elbow.

Science Skill

A model of an object can show how the real object works.

Your Bones and Muscles

Under your skin are hundreds of bones and muscles. Your bones and muscles work together. They help you sit, stand, walk, run, and move in many other ways.

muscles

bones

What Your Bones Do

Your bones fit together to make your **skeleton**. Your skeleton holds up your body and gives it shape.

Some bones help you move. Other bones protect parts inside your body. Your ribs protect your heart and lungs. Your skull protects your brain.

■ **Which bones help you move?**

arm bones

hand bones

skull

ribs

spine, or backbone

hip bones

leg bones

foot bones

What Your Muscles Do

Your **muscles** are body parts that work to move your bones and do other jobs. Your heart is a muscle that pumps blood through your body.

arm muscles

shoulder muscles

stomach muscles

chest muscles

leg muscles

■ What muscles is the boy using to move?

Your Bones and Muscles Work Together

Muscles work in pairs to move your bones. One muscle pulls a bone to move it. Then the other muscle pulls the bone to move it back.

■ How do this boy's muscles move his leg bones?

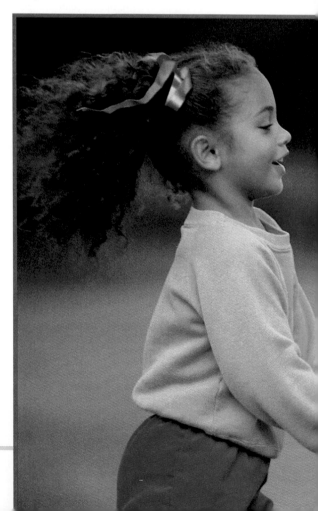

Keeping Bones and Muscles Healthy

You can keep your bones and muscles strong and healthy. Exercising every day helps your bones and muscles stay strong. Eating healthful food keeps them healthy.

■ How are these children keeping their bones and muscles strong and healthy?

Think About It

1. How do your bones and muscles work together?
2. How can you keep your bones and muscles strong and healthy?

How Do My Heart and Lungs Work?

 Investigate

A Heartbeat

You will need

paper cup
with bottom cut out

1 Work with a partner. Your partner will use the cup to listen to your heartbeat.

2 Jump up and down while your partner counts to 10.

3 Your partner will observe your heartbeat again. Is it faster or slower? Trade places.

Science Skill
When you observe, you may use tools along with your senses.

Your Heart and Lungs

Your heart and lungs help keep you alive. Your **heart** is a muscle that pumps blood to every part of your body. Your **lungs** are body parts that help you breathe the air you need to live.

■ How can you tell that your heart and lungs work harder when you exercise?

A55

How Your Heart Works

Your heart is about the size of your fist. Each time your heart beats, it pumps blood to all the parts of your body.

Your **heart rate** is how fast or slowly your heart beats. When you exercise, your heart beats faster. Your heart rate is faster. When you rest, your heart rate is slower.

■ **In what part of your body is your heart?**

How Your Lungs Work

You have two lungs inside your chest. Air goes in and out of your lungs when you breathe. When you breathe in, the air moves down a tube into your lungs. Your lungs fill with air and get larger. When you breathe out, air leaves your lungs.

■ Compare the inside and outside of a lung. How are they different?

Your Heart and Lungs Work Together

Your heart and lungs work together to get your body the oxygen it needs. Your heart pumps blood first to your lungs. Your lungs take in oxygen from the air you breathe. The blood picks up the oxygen and takes it back to your heart. Then your heart pumps the blood to all parts of your body.

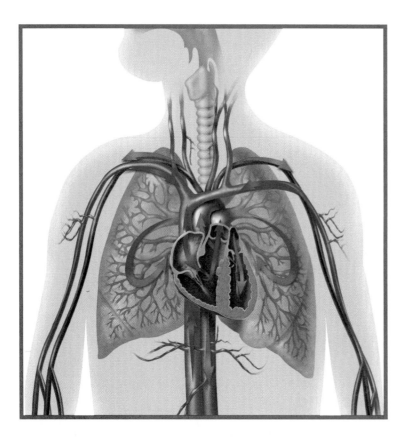

■ How does blood get to your lungs? Where does it go after that?

When the blood comes back to your heart, it is pumped to your lungs again for more oxygen.

■ How is this boy keeping his
heart and lungs healthy?

Keeping Your Heart and Lungs Healthy

It is important to keep your heart and lungs healthy. Exercise helps your heart and lungs as well as your bones and muscles. When you exercise, your heart and lungs work harder and get stronger.

Think About It

1. How do your heart and lungs work together?
2. How can you keep your heart and lungs healthy?

How Do I Digest Food?

Investigate

How Digestion Begins

You will need

cracker

mirror

paper and pencil

1 Observe the cracker. Draw it.

2 Put the cracker in your mouth. Do not chew it. Count slowly to 20.

3 Think about how the cracker feels. Use the mirror to observe it.

4 Draw what you observe. Tell what you think is happening.

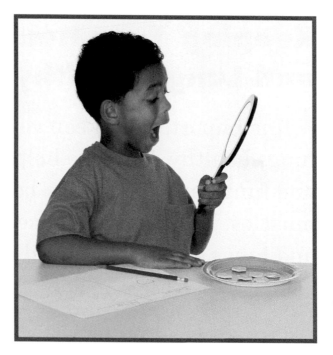

Science Skill
You can use a mirror to help you observe.

How Your Body Digests Food

Healthful food has the energy and nutrients your body needs to grow and stay healthy. To get the energy and nutrients, your body must **digest**, or break down, the food.

mouth

tube to the stomach

stomach

small intestine

large intestine

How Your Body Digests Food

Your body starts to digest food in your mouth. When you chew your food, it mixes with saliva. **Saliva** is the liquid in your mouth that begins to break down food.

When you swallow the food you have chewed, it goes down a tube. Muscles in the tube push the food to your stomach.

mouth

tube to the stomach

■ **Where does your body start to digest food?**

Your **stomach** is like a bag made of muscles. The muscles squeeze the food and mix it with special juices. The food turns into a thick liquid.

The liquid food moves into your small intestine. From there, the nutrients from the food go into your blood. Your blood carries the nutrients to all parts of your body. Food parts that your body does not need move into your large intestine.

mouth

tube to the stomach

stomach

small intestine

large intestine

Eating Healthful Foods

Healthful foods keep you healthy. They help your body grow and give you energy. Eating just one kind of food will not give your body everything it needs. You should eat different kinds of foods every day.

The Food Guide Pyramid can help you choose healthful foods. You need foods from each group. The foods you should eat the most of are at the bottom. The foods you should eat the least of are at the top.

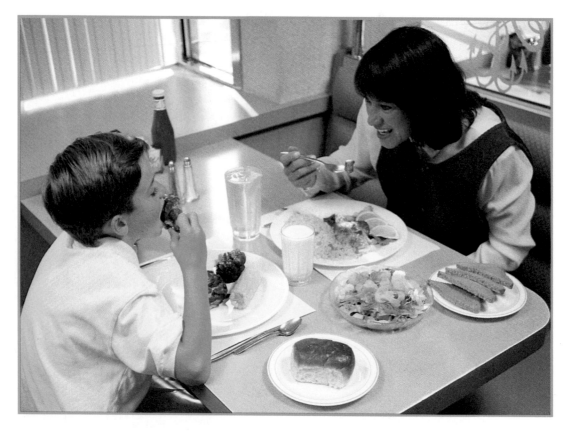

■ What healthful foods are the boy and his mother eating?

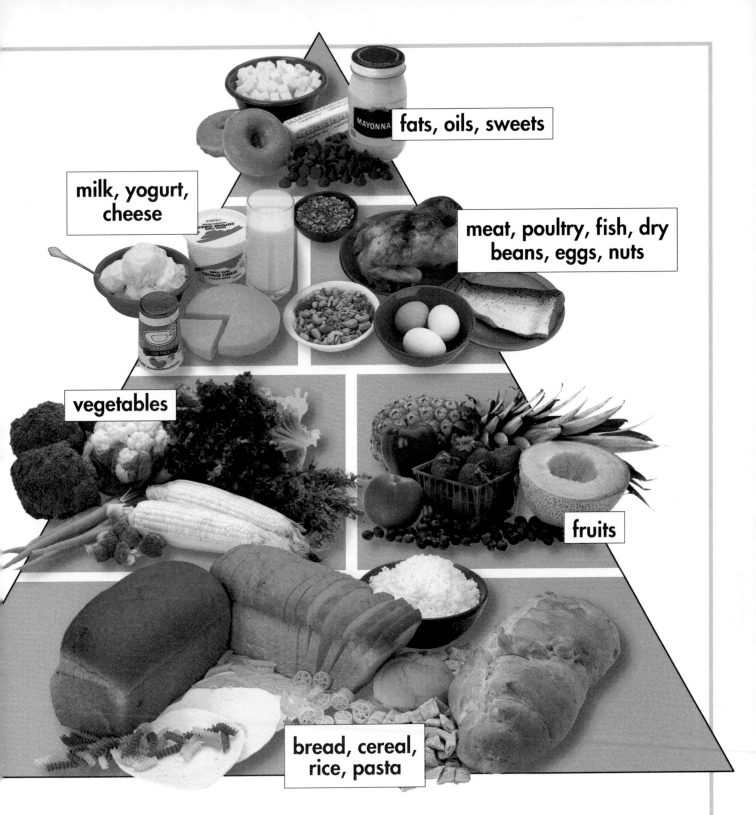

fats, oils, sweets

milk, yogurt, cheese

meat, poultry, fish, dry beans, eggs, nuts

vegetables

fruits

bread, cereal, rice, pasta

Think About It

1. How does your body digest food?
2. What are some healthful foods?

Math Link

How Many Hand Bones?

Your wrist, palm, and fingers are all parts of your hand. Each part has many bones. You can see them in this picture. There are 8 bones in your wrist and 5 bones in your palm. There are ⑭ bones in your fingers.

hand X ray

Think and Do

Trace your hand. Then draw in the bones. Write an addition problem to show how many bones there are in all.

A School Nurse Communicates with Students

School nurses and health aides help keep you healthy. This nurse is checking to see that this boy is growing well. A nurse also checks weight and height. He or she may take care of you when you are ill.

Think and Do

Write some questions you would like to ask a school nurse about keeping healthy. Invite your school nurse or health aide to visit your class. Get answers to your questions.

Tell What You Know

1. Use the pictures to tell how people grow and change.

Vocabulary

Use the terms in the box to tell about each picture.

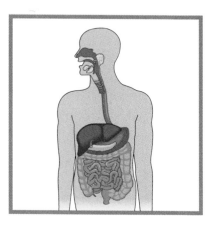

2. permanent teeth

skeleton

muscles

3. heart

heart rate

lungs

4. digest

saliva

stomach

Using Science Skills

5. **Observe** People can do things to make themselves healthier and stronger. For two days, observe what you do to be healthy. Make a list of your observations. Then use your list to talk about how you help yourself be healthy.

6. **Compare** Look at a baby picture of yourself. Then make a chart like this one. How are you the same and different now?

Me		
	As a Baby	Now
Hair Color	light Brown	Black
Eye Color	Brown	Brown
Teeth	x	Cricked
Other Things	little legs	

Grow a Sweet Potato

1. Stick toothpicks into a sweet potato. Place the sweet potato in a jar of water.

2. Put the jar in a sunny place.

3. Observe the sweet potato for a month.

4. Draw pictures to show how the sweet potato grows and changes.

Observe Differences Between Dogs

1. Look through magazines and books for pictures of dogs.

2. Observe the dogs, and make a list of the ways they look different from one another.

3. Compare your list with the lists of classmates.

How Dogs
Are Different

Size

Color

Measure Shoe Lengths

1. Trace your shoe and the shoe of an adult.

2. Measure how long each drawing is. Write the two measurements.

3. Subtract to find the difference between the two.

4. Infer what happens to children's feet over time.

Observe a Plant Without Leaves

1. Take all the leaves off a small plant.

2. Set the plant in a sunny place, and keep the plant watered.

3. Predict what will happen.

4. Observe the plant every day.

5. Draw pictures to show what happens.

WRITING
Sequence Game
Choose a plant or an animal. Draw and write about how it grows. Put one or more of your steps behind a flap for classmates to guess.

READING
Big Blue Whale
by Nicola Davies
How does the largest mammal on Earth grow and change? Read this book to find out.

 COMPUTER CENTER
Visit *The Learning Site* at
www.harcourtschool.com/ca

Exploring Earth's Surface

Earth Science

Exploring Earth's Surface

UNIT PROJECT

What Do You Know?

Make fossil flash cards. Write
questions on one side and
answers on the other side.

Earth's Resources

Vocabulary

rock

soil

boulder

sand

resource

natural resource

transportation

mineral

Did You Know?

In Hawaii, the black **sand** on some beaches is made up of pieces of **rock** from a nearby volcano.

Did You Know?

Diamond is a **mineral** that is so hard it can scratch glass.

How Do People Use Rocks and Soil?

Investigate

A Way to Use Soil

You will need

clay

ice cube tray

1 Fill an ice cube tray with clay. The clay will form bricks.

2 Put the tray in a warm, sunny place. Take the bricks out when they are hard.

3 What happened to the bricks? Infer why this happened.

Science Skill

When you infer information, you can figure out why something happened.

Ways That People Use Rocks and Soil

A **rock** is a hard, nonliving thing that comes from the Earth. The loose top layer of the Earth's surface is **soil**. People use rocks and soil in different ways.

B5

Different Kinds of Rocks

Rocks have different sizes, colors, and shapes. A **boulder** is a large rock. A grain of **sand** is a tiny rock. A rock can be shiny or dull, and it can be smooth or rough. Some rocks are harder than others.

boulder

marble

pumice

granite

basalt

sandstone

obsidian

■ How are these rocks different?

Ways That People Use Rocks

Rocks are a kind of natural resource. A **resource** is anything that people can use. A **natural resource** is something found in nature that people can use to meet their needs.

People use rocks to build things, such as houses and roads. They also use rocks to make sculptures.

People may change the size, shape, and texture, or feel, of rocks. They break big rocks into smaller rocks to make gravel for roads. They make parts of sculptures rough and smooth.

Mount Rushmore

truck dumping gravel

■ How are the rocks in the truck being used?

Kinds of Soil

Different kinds of soil have different things in them. Sandy soil has a lot of sand in it. Topsoil has many bits of dead plants and animals. Clay soil is made up of tiny pieces of rock that stick together easily. The three kinds of soil hold different amounts of water.

■ **Which kind of soil holds the most water? Which kind holds the least?**

topsoil

clay soil

sandy soil

potato field

Ways That People Use Soil

People use soil to grow food and to make bricks. One kind of brick is called adobe. People make a mix of wet clay and straw and shape it into bricks. They use the hard bricks to build things.

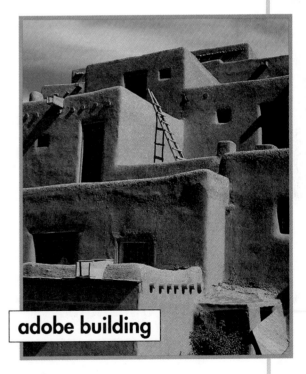

adobe building

Think About It

1. How do people use rocks?
2. How do people use soil?

How Do People Use Water?

Investigate

How You Use Water

How Our Class Uses Water in One Day	
How Our Class Uses Water	How Many Times
drinking	
washing hands	
watering plants	
cleaning	

1 Keep track of the ways your class uses water in one day. Collect the data in a chart.

2 Make a tally mark each time your class uses water. After a day, count the marks.

3 Use your data to answer these questions.
- How many ways did your class use water?
- Which way did your class use water most?

Science Skill

Collecting data is one way to find the answers to your questions.

Ways That People Use Water

Water is a natural resource that people use every day. People drink water, but they also use it for swimming, transportation, and cleaning. How are people using water here?

Uses for Water

People, plants, and animals need water to live and grow. People use water for drinking, cooking, bathing, and watering plants. They also use it for washing clothes, dishes, and cars.

■ **How are these children using water?**

ferry

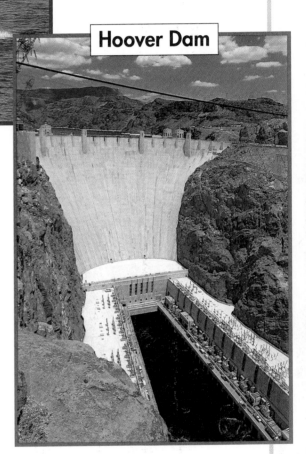

Hoover Dam

People also use water when they sail boats and ships. Boats and ships are kinds of **transportation**, or ways to move people or things.

Water is also used to make electricity. People build dams on rivers. The flow of the river turns machines that make electricity.

Think About It

1. How do people use water to care for plants and animals?
2. What are some other ways people use water?

B13

What Other Natural Resources Do People Use?

Investigate

Using Plants to Make a Bird Feeder

You will need

milk carton   scissors   plant parts   glue   birdseed

1. With your teacher, cut the top off a milk carton.

   CAUTION Cut carefully.

2. Glue plant parts to the sides and bottom of the carton.

3. Put birdseed in your feeder, and place it outside.

4. Communicate to classmates what you did.

Science Skill
You can show things to communicate about them.

Other Natural Resources People Use

Plants and air are two other important natural resources. People use these natural resources to meet their needs. How are these people using plants and air?

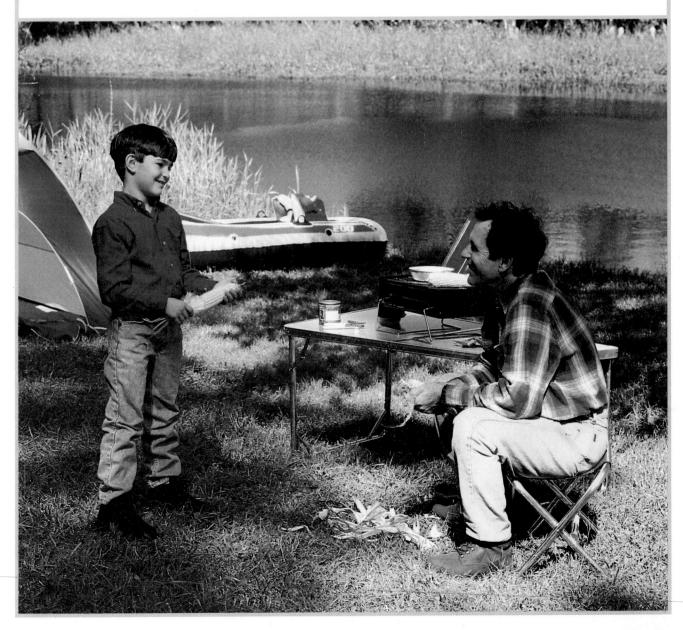

How People Use Plants

Plants are a resource that people use to make many products. People use wood from trees to build furniture and houses.

pine stool

pine tree

People also use wood as fuel. Fuel is something that is burned to make heat. People can use heat from burning wood to stay warm and to cook. They can also use it to make tools and clay pots.

firewood

cotton boll

cotton hat

People also make cloth from plants. They use the cotton plant to make cloth for clothes, sheets, and many other products.

People also use plants for food. They eat fruits and vegetables. They use other plant parts to make foods such as bread and pasta.

■ **How is this boy using plants?**

How People Use Air

Air is another important resource. People need clean air to breathe, but they use it in other ways, too. They use air to fill tires, rafts, and toys. They also use air when they fly in airplanes.

Where People Find Minerals

Minerals are another natural resource people use. A **mineral** is one kind of nonliving thing that is found in nature. Minerals are found in rocks. Most rocks have two or more kinds of minerals in them.

quartz

Gneiss

biotite

Granite

pink feldspar

biotite

quartz

■ How are these two rocks different?

How People Use Minerals

People have found many uses for minerals. Copper, topaz, and iron come from minerals. People use materials from minerals to make coins, jewelry, and furniture.

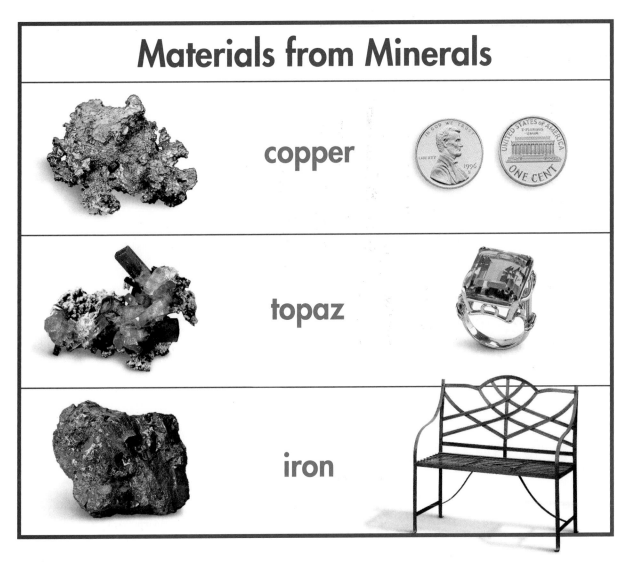

Materials from Minerals

	copper	
	topaz	
	iron	

Think About It

1. What are some ways people use plants?
2. What are some other resources people use?

Math Link

How Much Water?

Most people use about 100 gallons of water each day. They use the water for <u>drinking</u>, keeping <u>clean</u>, and <u>cooking</u>. They also use it for <u>washing</u> clothes, <u>dishes</u>, <u>and pets</u>.

Think and Do

It takes about 2 gallons of water to wash your hands and face. If 4 people in a family wash their hands and faces, how much water will they use? Write an addition problem to show the answer.

4 people in the family

2
+

An Artist Uses Natural Resources

Maya Lin is an architect and artist who works with stone and other natural materials. She has designed sculptures made of granite and has even used water in her work. Lin designed an earth sculpture called "The Wave Field." It is made of soil covered with grass.

Think and Do

Design your own sculpture. First draw a picture of what your sculpture will look like. Use rocks, clay, soil, leaves and other natural materials to make your sculpture.

Tell What You Know

1. How does the picture show ways people use natural resources?

Vocabulary

Tell which picture best goes with each word.

2. mineral

3. boulder

4. soil

5. sand

a.

b.

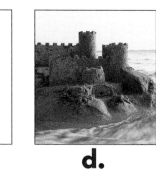
c.

d.

Using Science Skills

6. Make Models/Communicate

Make a model boat to show one way people use water. Decide what you will use to make your model. You could use clay, paper, or an empty milk carton.

Write one sentence that tells how your model boat uses water. Write another sentence that tells what resources you used to make it.

7. Collect Data/Communicate

Make a chart to show ways people use three resources. Draw or cut out pictures that show some ways that each resource is used. Glue your pictures in the chart. Then share your chart.

How People Use Resources		
Rocks	Plants	Soil

Earth Long Ago

Vocabulary

fossil
paleontologist
reconstruct
dinosaur
extinct
Triceratops

Did You Know?
Plant-eating **dinosaurs** were the largest land animals that ever lived on Earth.

Did You Know?

The moa was a bird 10 feet tall that became **extinct** about 300 years ago.

What Is a Fossil?

How Some Fossils Get Their Shapes

You will need

clay

small objects

1 Break the clay into four pieces. Press each piece flat.

2 Press a different object into each piece to make a print. Remove the object.

3 Have classmates infer which object made each print.

Science Skill
You can use clues to infer information.

Fossils

Plants and animals lived on the Earth before people did. People know this because they have found fossils. A **fossil** is what is left of a plant or an animal that lived long ago.

fossil

How Fossils Are Made

Some plants and animals that died millions of years ago were eaten. Many rotted away. Other plants and animals became fossils.

These pictures show one way fossils are made. A fish in the ocean dies. Its body sinks to the ocean floor. Soon the fish is covered up with mud.

fish fossil

■ **What is happening to the fish's body?**

How a Fossil Is Made

1 A fish dies.

2 Mud and sand cover the fish.

A **paleontologist** is a scientist who finds and studies fossils. By studying fossils, a paleontologist learns about plants and animals that lived long ago.

More mud and sand cover the fish's body as it rots away. They press on the mud for a long time until this mud turns to rock. A print of the fish is left in the rock. Prints like this are one kind of fossil.

3 The mud and sand turn to rock.

- **What is this paleontologist doing?**

Where Fossils Are Found

Scientists find many kinds of fossils in rocks. Some are animal teeth, shells, and bones that have turned to stone. Others are plant and animal prints.

footprint fossil

bird fossil

■ What kind of fossil is this?

Scientists also find fossils in other things, such as tar and amber. Amber is the hard sap of pine trees that grew long ago.

fly in amber

saber-toothed cat fossil

mammoth fossil

Think About It

1. How are some fossils made?
2. Where are some fossils found?

How Do Scientists Get Fossils?

How Scientists Find Fossils

You will need

play dough   small objects   tools

1 Hide an object in some play dough. Let the dough get hard. Trade with a classmate.

2 Use tools to find the object. Do not harm the object.

3 Communicate what you did.

Science Skill
One way to **communicate** is to talk with your partner about what you did.

How Scientists Get Fossils

Scientists find some fossils inside rocks. To get the fossils out, they must chip the rock away. They work slowly and carefully so that they do not break the fossils.

How Scientists Put Fossils Together

When scientists chip a fossil from a rock, it may be in pieces. They take the fossil pieces to a museum, where they first clean them.

Then the scientists try to put the fossil together. They look at the pieces and use what they know about animals. They want to **reconstruct**, or rebuild, as much of the skeleton as possible.

Putting Fossils Together

 The fossil is taken out of the rock.

 The pieces are cleaned.

What Scientists Learn from Fossils

Afrovenator fossil

Fossils help scientists learn about plants and animals that lived long ago. Scientists also learn from fossils how plants and animals have changed. They compare the fossils with plants and animals that live today.

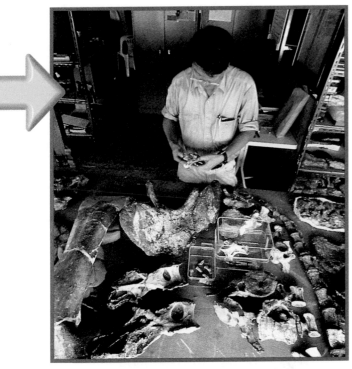

③ The fossil pieces are put together.

■ Observe the fossil above. How do you think the living animal looked?

Think About It

1. How do scientists get fossils?
2. What do scientists learn from fossils?

What Have Scientists Learned About Dinosaurs?

Investigate

Dinosaur Skeletons

You will need

scissors

books about dinosaurs

chenille sticks

1. Choose a dinosaur to make a model skeleton.

2. Twist two chenille sticks together. Shape them to make the backbone and the head.

3. Twist sticks around the backbone for legs. Cut and twist on more sticks for ribs.

   CAUTION Cut carefully.

Science Skill
Sharing your model can help you explain your ideas.

What Scientists Know About Dinosaurs

A **dinosaur** is an animal that lived millions of years ago. Today dinosaurs are **extinct**, or no longer living. Paleontologists know about dinosaurs from their fossils.

dinosaur fossil

Kinds of Dinosaurs

Many kinds of dinosaurs used to live on the Earth. Some were as small as a chicken. Others were taller than a three-story building.

The word *dinosaur* means "terrible lizard." Paleontologists give each dinosaur a name that describes it. One kind of dinosaur is named **Triceratops**, which means "three-horned face."

Another dinosaur is named Tyrannosaurus rex. Its name means "tyrant lizard king." A tyrant is a mean ruler. Tyrannosaurus rex was one of the fiercest dinosaurs of all.

How Tall Were Dinosaurs?

Stegosaurus   Triceratops

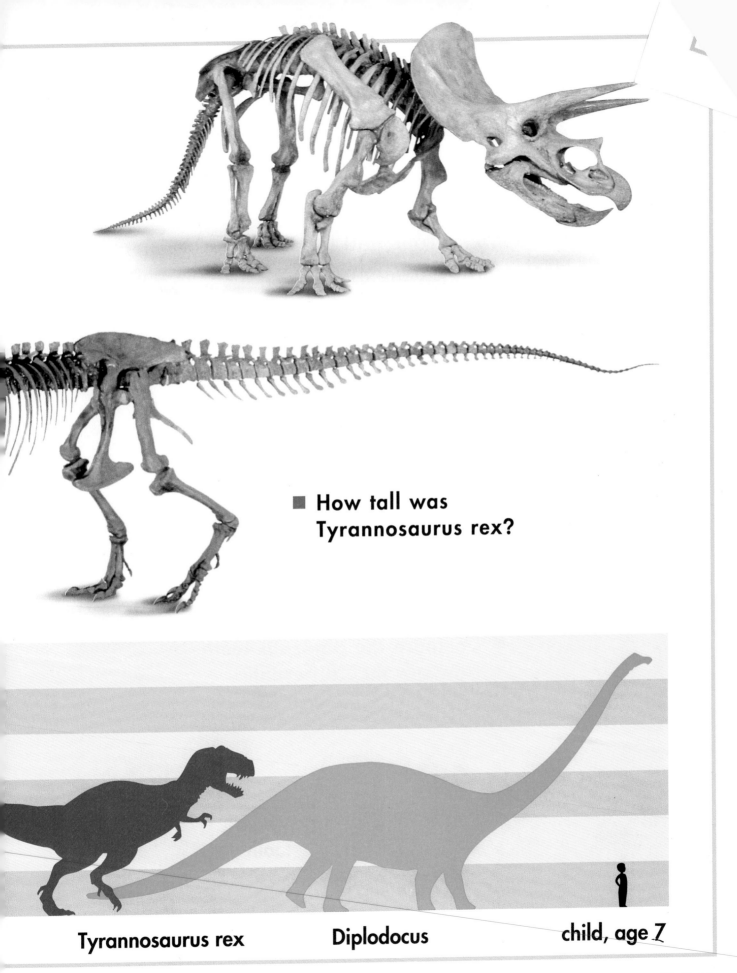

■ **How tall was Tyrannosaurus rex?**

Tyrannosaurus rex   Diplodocus   child, age 7

What Scientists Learn About Dinosaurs

One way paleontologists learn about dinosaurs is by comparing them to animals that live today. Triceratops had flat teeth like those of today's plant-eating animals. Tyrannosaurus rex had long, pointed teeth like those of today's meat eaters.

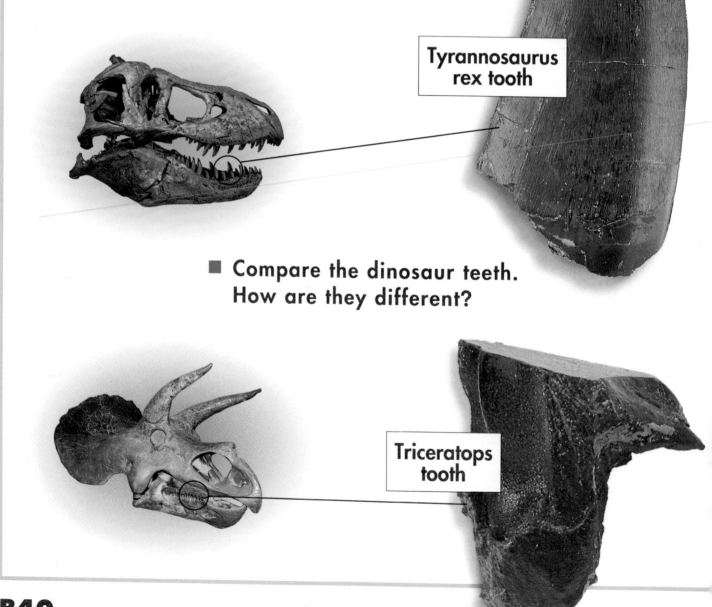

Tyrannosaurus rex tooth

■ Compare the dinosaur teeth. How are they different?

Triceratops tooth

Scientists have found fossil prints of dinosaur skin. These fossils show that some dinosaurs had scaly skin. Others had smoother skin.

dinosaur skin

Scientists know that some dinosaurs laid eggs. Fossil dinosaur nests have been found with fossils of eggs in them. Scientists have also found fossils of young dinosaurs around some nests.

■ **What is in this dinosaur nest?**

Think About It

1. How do scientists learn about dinosaurs?

2. What have scientists found out about dinosaurs?

Math Link

Compare Dinosaur Sizes

Scientists know from fossils that dinosaurs were many sizes. Compsognathus was about 2 feet long. Scelidosaurus was about 12 feet long. Stegosaurus was larger. It was about 20 feet long.

Compsognathus

Scelidosaurus

Stegosaurus

Think and Do

Make a bar graph to compare the lengths of these dinosaurs. Then use your graph to talk about which dinosaur was the longest and which was the shortest.

No More Brontosaurus

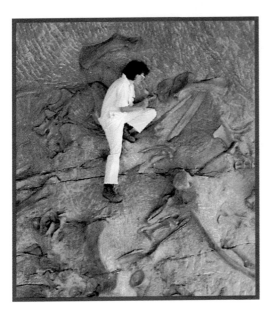

Paleontologists found fossils of a kind of dinosaur they named Apatosaurus. Then they found bone fossils that looked the same but were bigger. They thought they had found a different kind of dinosaur and called it Brontosaurus.

Later, scientists figured out that both sets of fossils were from Apatosaurus bones. The name Brontosaurus is not used anymore.

Think and Do

Find out what it might be like to fit fossils together. Draw two pictures of the same kind of animal, but make one larger. Cut out each body part. Mix up the body parts of both animals. Trade with a classmate. Try to put each of your classmate's two pictures together.

Tell What You Know

1. Tell what you know about each picture.

Vocabulary

Use these words to tell about the picture.

2. fossil

3. dinosaur

4. extinct

5. Triceratops

6. paleontologist

Using Science Skills

7. **Make a Model** This is a trilobite fossil. A trilobite was an animal that lived in the ocean millions of years ago. It was about 8 to 10 centimeters, or 3 to 4 inches, long.

   Use clay and a pencil tip to make a model of a trilobite fossil. Use your model to tell a classmate about trilobites.

8. **Infer** The table shows the teeth of two dinosaurs. Copy the table. Write what each dinosaur ate and how you know.

Dinosaur Teeth and What Dinosaurs Ate			
Dinosaur	Shape of Tooth	What It Ate	How I Know
Tyrannosaurus			
Triceratops			

Weather Some Rocks

1. Put some small rocks in a plastic jar.

2. Add 250 milliliters of water to the jar, and put the lid on. Look at the bottom of the jar. Record what you see.

3. Shake the jar 100 times. Look at the bottom of the jar again. Record what you see.

4. Infer what happened to the rocks.

Look for Fossils

1. Press some clay into a flat layer. This is a layer of "rock."

2. Press pieces of pasta into the clay. These are "fossils."

3. Add more layers of rocks and more layers of fossils.

4. Cut through the layers with a craft stick. Can you find the fossils? yes

Grow Plants in Soil

1. Punch holes in each cup. Label the cups.

2. Fill each cup with different amounts of peat moss, sand, and clay.

3. Plant 3 seeds in each cup. Put the cups in a sunny place. Keep the seeds watered.

4. In two weeks, record the height of the plants. Which combination of soils was best for growing the plants?

Classify Rocks

light colored rocks

dark colored rocks

1. Collect some small rocks.

2. Observe the rocks and decide how you want to classify them.

3. Glue the rocks in groups on pieces of cardboard. Label each group.

4. Share your rocks with classmates.

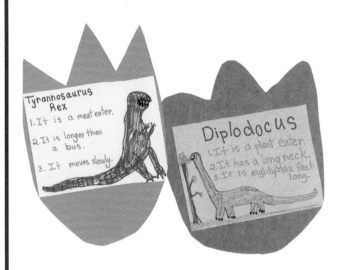

WRITING

Track Facts Choose a dinosaur to learn more about. Write facts. Draw its picture on a dinosaur footprint. Add your writing to a class "dinosaur trail."

READING

Fossils Tell of Long Ago by Aliki

What kinds of fossils have people found on mountains? Share what you learn.

COMPUTER CENTER
Visit *The Learning Site* at www.harcourtschool.com/ca

Matter and Motion

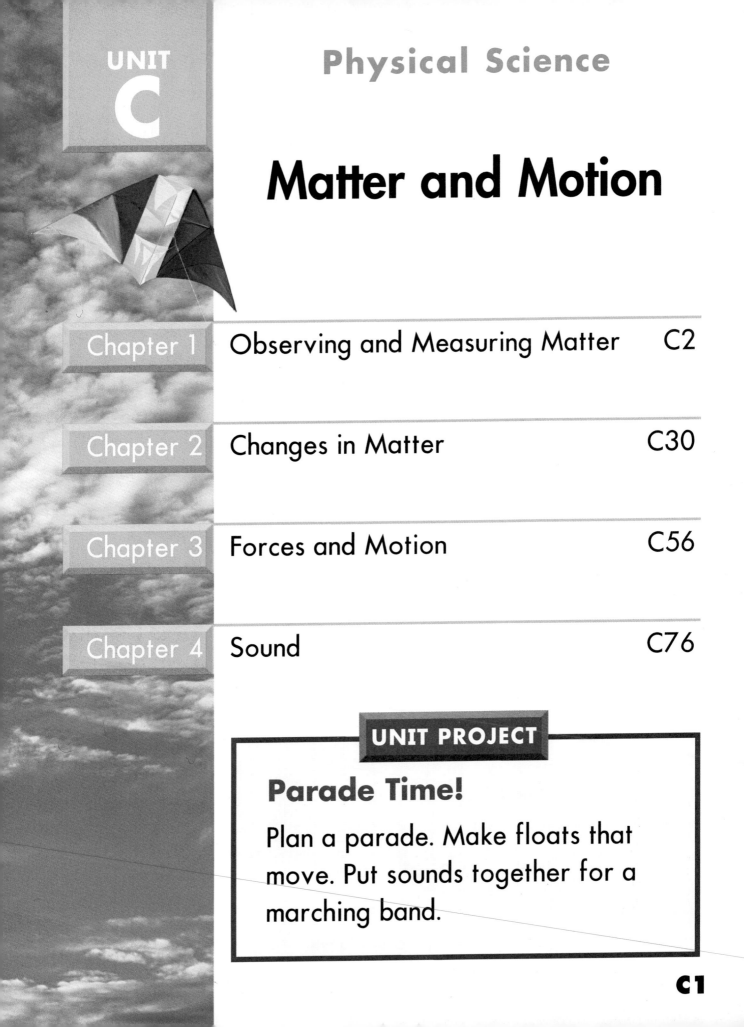

Matter and Motion

UNIT PROJECT

Parade Time!

Plan a parade. Make floats that move. Put sounds together for a marching band.

Observing and Measuring Matter

Vocabulary

matter

property

mass

solid

centimeter

liquid

milliliter

gas

Did You Know?

A **gas** called propane is burned to heat the air in a hot-air balloon.

Did You Know?

A **solid** that weighs 100 pounds on Earth would weigh only 17 pounds on the moon.

ON EARTH

ON THE MOON

What Is Matter?

Investigate

Matter

You will need

3 balls or markers

paper and pencil

1 Observe how the objects are alike and different.

2 Think of ways to classify the objects. Write your ideas.

3 Choose one way to classify the objects into groups.

4 Explain to a classmate how you classified the objects.

Science Skill
When you classify, you look for ways that things are alike, and then you put them into that group.

Matter

Matter is what all things are made of. Trees, milk, and air are all made of matter. Even you are made of matter! What different kinds of matter do you see here?

Forms of Matter

Matter has three forms. It can be a solid, a liquid, or a gas. The party hats, the bowl, and the chair are solids. The juice in the bowl is a liquid. The air in the balloons is a gas.

solids

- **How are the objects on these two pages alike and different?**

liquid

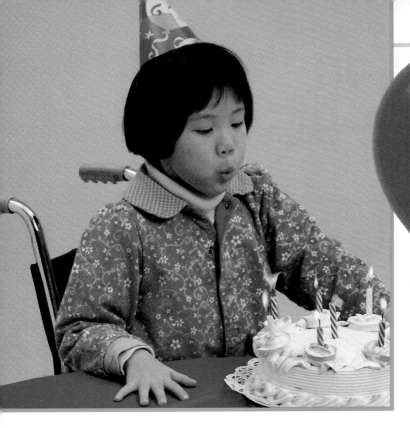

gas

Properties of Matter

Matter has certain properties. A **property** is a quality of something. Color, size, and shape are properties of matter.

Two other properties of matter are that it takes up space and that it has mass. An object's **mass** is the amount of matter it has.

Think About It

1. What is matter, and what are its forms?
2. What are some properties of matter?

What Can We Find Out About Solids?

Solids

You will need

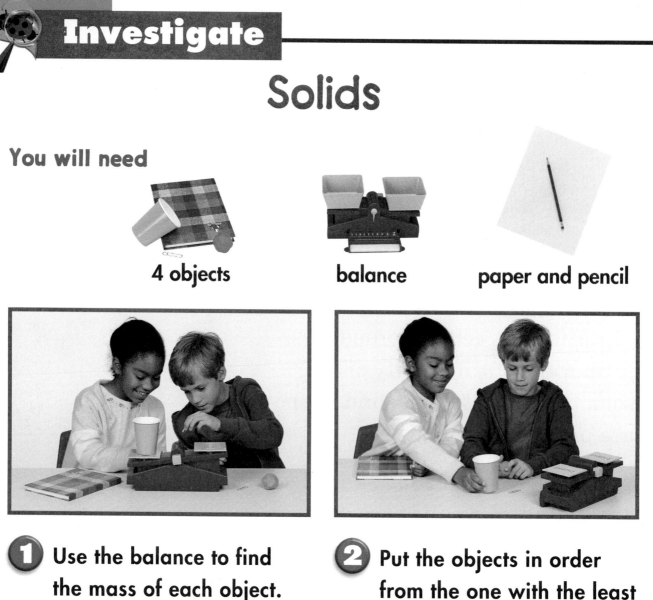

4 objects   balance   paper and pencil

1 Use the balance to find the mass of each object.

2 Put the objects in order from the one with the least mass to the one with the most mass.

3 Make a chart that shows the objects in order from the one with the least mass to the one with the most mass.

Science Skill

When you put objects in order, you can arrange them from least to most.

Solids

A solid is one kind of matter. Like all matter, it takes up space and has mass. A **solid** is the only form of matter that has a shape of its own.

Finding Out About Solids

All the objects you see here are solids. They are different in color, size, and shape. They have different textures. A texture is the way something feels.

Solids are alike in some important ways. Each one has its own size and shape. A solid will not change in size or shape unless you do something such as cut, bend, or break it.

■ **How are these objects alike and different?**

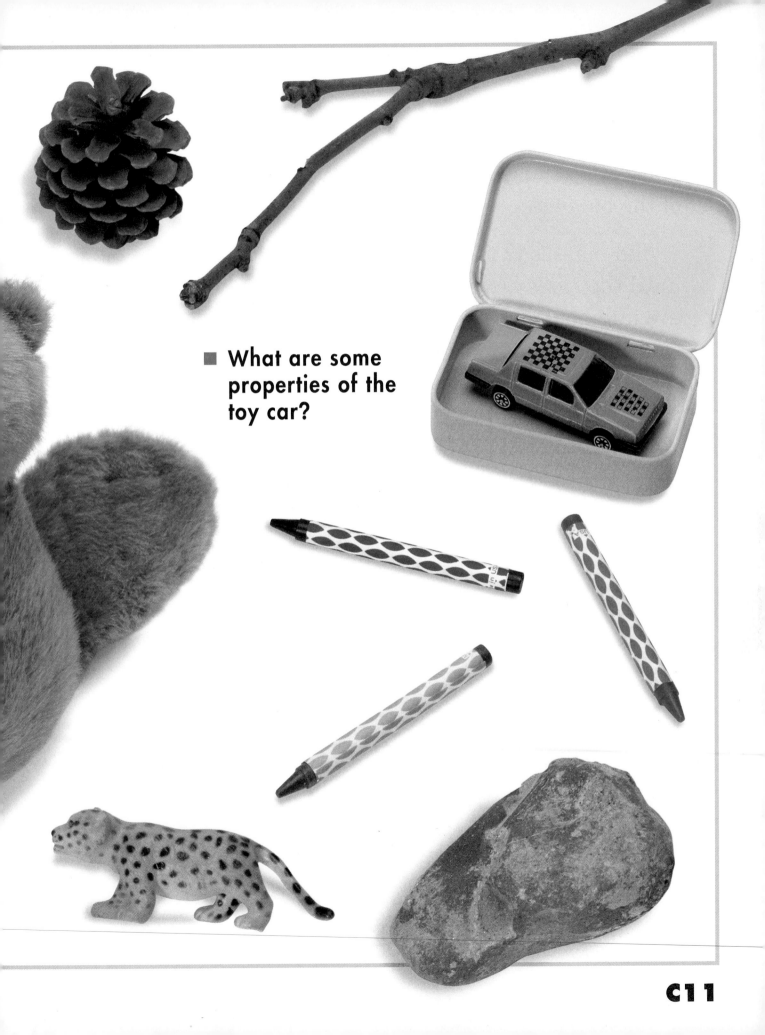

What are some properties of the toy car?

C11

Measuring Solids

A balance can help you find out the mass of a solid. Put the solid on one side of the balance.

Add masses to the other side until the sides are even. There are numbers on the masses. Add them to find how much mass equals the mass of the solid.

■ **What is this girl using to measure the mass of the toy?**

You can measure how long or wide a solid is. You can also measure how big around it is.

A **centimeter** is a unit used to measure length. You can use centimeters to find the length of a solid.

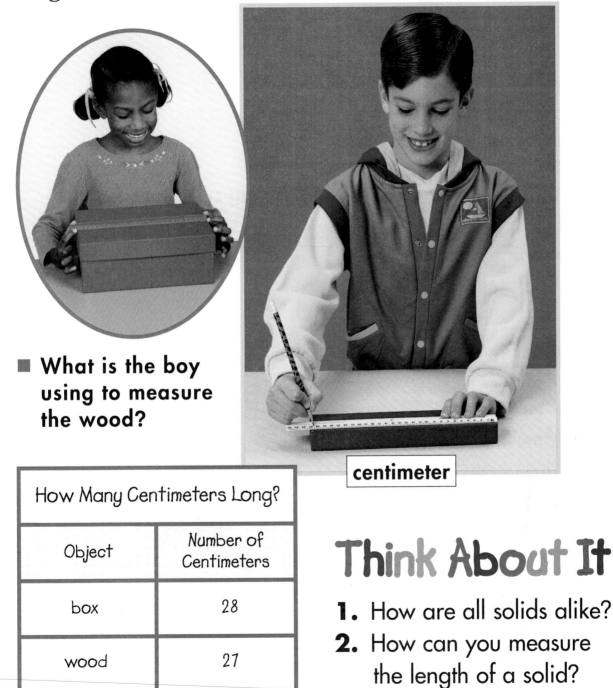

■ **What is the boy using to measure the wood?**

centimeter

How Many Centimeters Long?	
Object	Number of Centimeters
box	28
wood	27

Think About It

1. How are all solids alike?

2. How can you measure the length of a solid?

What Can We Find Out About Liquids?

Liquids

You will need

marker

3 colors of water

measuring cup

3 containers

1. Draw a line at the same height on all 3 containers. Pour water into each container to the line.

2. Pour the water from one container into the empty measuring cup. Measure, and record the amount.

3. Repeat Step 2 for the other containers.

4. Compare the numbers. What can you infer?

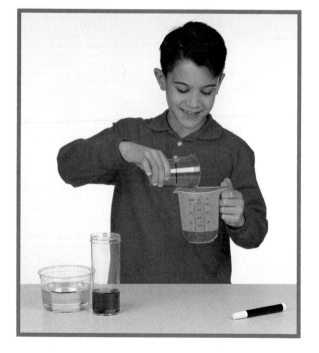

Science Skill

You can use a measuring cup to measure the amount of a liquid.

Liquids

A **liquid** is a form of matter that does not have its own shape. It flows to take the shape of its container. Like a solid, a liquid takes up space and has mass. You can see and feel a liquid.

Finding Out About Liquids

The liquid in a bottle has the same shape as the bottle. As you tilt the bottle, the liquid changes shape. If the liquid is poured from the bottle into a glass, it takes the shape of the glass.

■ **What shape has the honey taken?**

A liquid does not change in amount unless you add more or take some away. If you pour it into a glass, the amount of liquid stays the same.

■ **How has the shape of the lemonade changed here?**

Measuring Liquids

Like solids, liquids have mass. A container with liquid in it has more mass than the same container with no liquid. You can measure the mass of a liquid by putting it on a pan balance.

■ **Which cup has more mass? How do you know?**

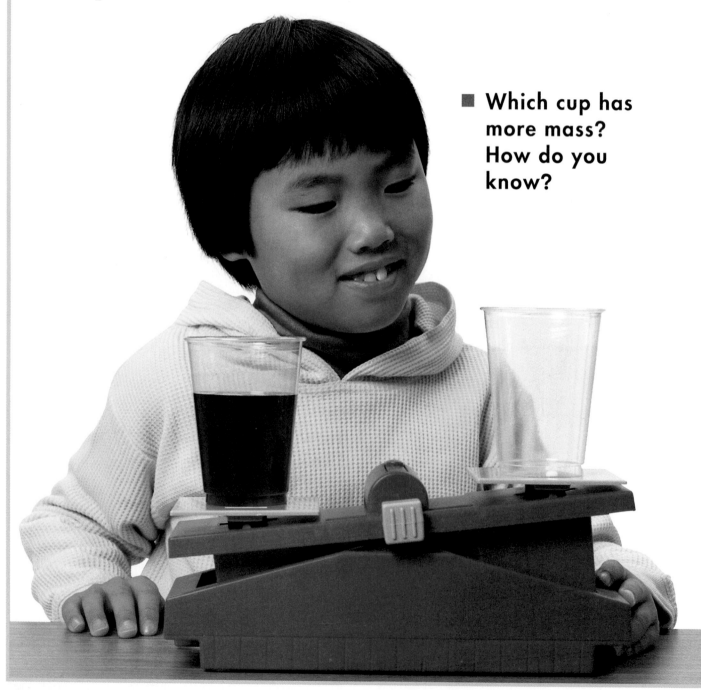

You can also measure the volume of a liquid. Volume is the amount of space a liquid takes up. A **milliliter** is a unit used to measure the volume of a liquid.

Volume in Milliliters	
Liquid	Number of Milliliters
apple juice	75 milliliters
orange juice	150 milliliters

Think About It

1. What are two properties of liquids?
2. How can you measure a liquid?

What Can We Find Out About Gases?

Investigate

Gases

You will need

water   cup   paper towel

1 Push a paper towel tightly into the bottom of the cup.

2 Turn the cup upside down. Push it straight down in the water.

3 Observe the cup. Is there water in it? Lift the cup straight up out of the water.

4 Infer what happened.

Science Skill
When you infer, you use what you know and what you observe to explain what happened.

Gases

Like all matter, gas takes up space and has mass. Like a liquid, a gas takes the shape of its container. A **gas** is the only kind of matter that always fills all the space inside a container.

The Shapes Gases Take

When you pump air into a soccer ball, the air spreads out inside. It fills the space of its container. The air takes the round shape of the ball.

■ **What shape is the air inside the bubble?**

Did You Know?
Air is a **mixture** of 11 different gases.

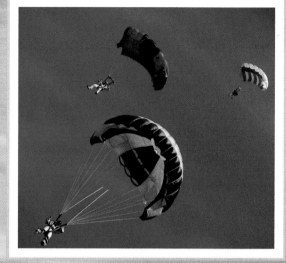

What Happens When You Mix Matter?

Investigate

Mixing Matter

You will need

 plastic knife

 nuts, seeds, dried fruit

 measuring cup

 zip-top bag

1 Cut up the dried fruit. Measure 100 milliliters each of nuts, seeds, and fruit.

2 Put the foods in the bag. Close the bag tightly and shake.

3 Observe. What has changed or not changed?

Science Skill

You can use more than one of your senses to observe something changing.

Cutting and Mixing Matter

Matter can be cut and mixed. When solid matter is cut, its shape changes, but its mass stays the same. When pieces of solid matter are mixed together, each piece stays the same.

Cutting and Shaping Matter

Cutting is just one way you can change matter. This loaf of bread is a solid. It has been cut into slices. The slices have a different shape from the loaf, but they are the same bread. Together, the slices have the same mass as the loaf.

■ How did the paper change when it was cut? How has it stayed the same?

If you change just the shape of matter, its mass stays the same. These two pieces of clay were once alike. They had the same shape and the same mass. Then the shape of one piece was changed, but its mass is still the same.

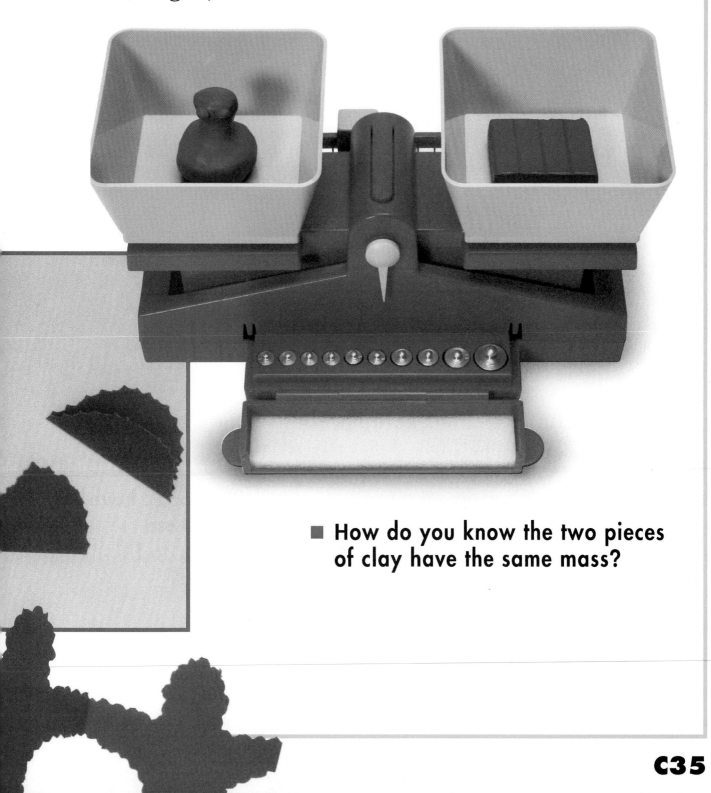

■ **How do you know the two pieces of clay have the same mass?**

Mixing Matter

When you put different kinds of matter together, you make a mixture. A **mixture** is something made up of two or more things. Things you put together in a mixture do not change.

A taco is filled with a mixture of beans, cheese, tomatoes, sauce, and lettuce. If you separate the foods in the mixture, you will find that they have not changed. For example, the beans are still beans.

■ **What foods have been mixed together to fill the taco?**

C36

■ **What kinds of things are in the jar? Why is this a mixture?**

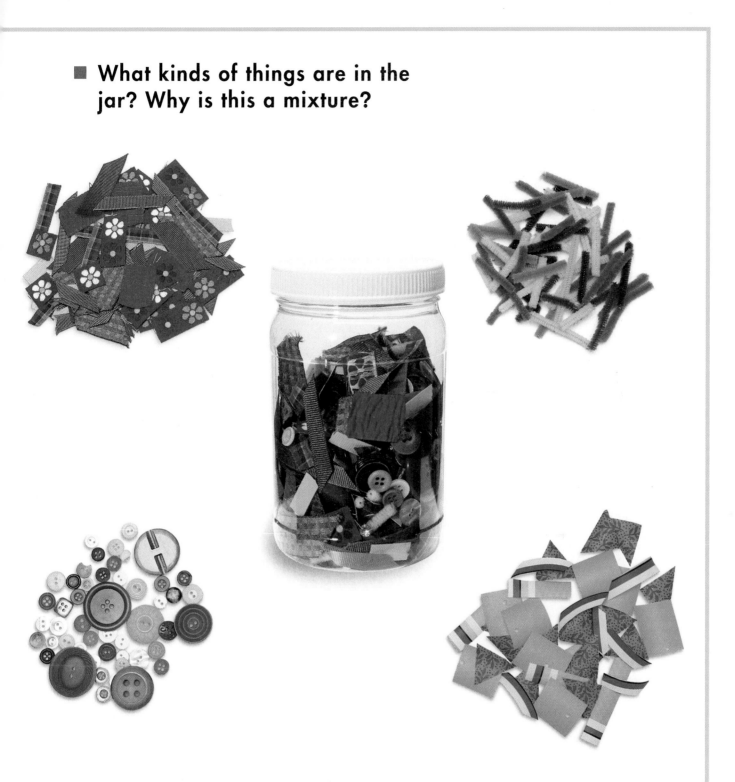

Think About It

1. What happens when you cut and shape matter?

2. What happens when you mix matter together?

How Can Water Change?

One Way That Water Changes

You will need

ice cubes

lamp

cloth

clock

1 Write about some ways to make an ice cube melt faster.

3 Record the time it takes each ice cube to melt.

4 Communicate to a classmate which way melted the ice faster.

2 Plan an investigation for two of the ways. Follow your plan.

CAUTION   Be careful if you use the lamp.

Science Skill
You can plan an investigation to see which way works the best.

How Water Can Change

Water can be a solid, a gas, or a liquid. Water as a solid may be ice or snow. Water as a gas is water vapor. In this picture, heat from the Earth is changing water from one form to another.

geysers,
Yellowstone National Park

Adding Heat Changes Water

Adding heat can make water change from one form of matter to another. Ice is water in its solid form. Water is a solid only when its temperature is 0°C or lower.

Adding heat raises the temperature of the ice. If the temperature goes above 0°C, the ice melts, or changes to a liquid.

■ **Why are the icicles melting?**

A puddle is liquid water. The sun's heat may cause the water in the puddle to evaporate, or change to water vapor.

When water gets hot enough, it boils, like the water in a kettle. When water boils, it evaporates.

■ **What makes liquid water turn into a gas?**

Taking Away Heat Changes Water

Taking away heat, or cooling, can also change the form of water. When enough heat is taken away from water, it freezes, or becomes a solid called ice. When enough heat is taken away from water vapor, it condenses, or becomes a liquid. Drops of liquid water form clouds and may fall as rain.

■ **How did the cloud form?**

Rain collects in lakes as liquid water. When the weather gets cold, the water freezes, or changes to ice. When the weather gets warm, the ice melts, or changes to liquid water.

Water changes from liquid to ice and back, and from liquid to vapor and back. All these changes are reversible. In a **reversible** change, matter can be changed back to the way it was.

■ How did the water in this lake change?

Think About It

1. What are the three forms of water?
2. What can make water change its form?

What Other Ways Does Matter Change?

A Mixture

You will need

½ cup of warm water   spoon   salt   pan

1 Mix one spoonful of salt into the water. Stir well.

2 Pour the mixture of salt and water into the pan.

3 Put the pan in a warm place. Predict what will happen.

4 Observe in two days. Did you predict correctly?

Science Skill

When you predict, you use what you know to make a good guess.

Other Ways Matter Changes

Matter can change in different ways. Some changes are reversible. Other changes are not reversible. How has the matter in this pizza changed?

Mixing and Shaping

You can mix together some things and then separate them again. Each thing will still be the same as it was before.

■ **Why is this mixture reversible?**

A change in shape can be reversible. A ball of clay sinks. You can change its shape to make it float, but it is still clay. You can change its shape back.

Gelatin must be changed before it is ready to eat. First, the solid powder is mixed with hot water. When the hot liquid mixture cools, it becomes firm. If the gelatin is heated, it begins to change back. Some of the gelatin melts and becomes liquid again.

■ **How can a gelatin dessert change?**

Burning and Cooking

Some changes to matter are **irreversible**, or not able to change back. In an irreversible change, matter cannot be changed back to the way it once was. Fire and high heat often cause irreversible changes.

Burning causes wood to change to ashes and smoke. The ashes, gases, and smoke cannot be changed back to wood again.

■ What irreversible change will this fire cause?

Cooking can also cause irreversible changes. Cooking makes an egg change from a liquid to a solid. It also makes the egg change in color, texture, and taste. You cannot do anything to make the cooked egg become raw, or uncooked, again.

■ **How did the egg change?**

Think About It

1. What are some changes in matter that are reversible?
2. What are some changes in matter that are irreversible?

Math Link

How Much Liquid Changes to a Gas?

You can use a measuring cup to find out how much liquid water changes into a gas.

Think and Do

Pour 100 mL of water into a measuring cup. Put the cup on a windowsill in the sun.

After three days, measure and record how much water is in the cup. Write a subtraction problem to figure out how much of the water evaporated, or changed to a gas.

Art Link

A Potter Changes the Shape of Matter

A potter uses clay to make beautiful things. This potter is shaping clay into a pot. He will put the clay pot in a special oven. The clay will change to a different kind of matter that is very hard. Some kinds of clay can get hard just by drying in the air.

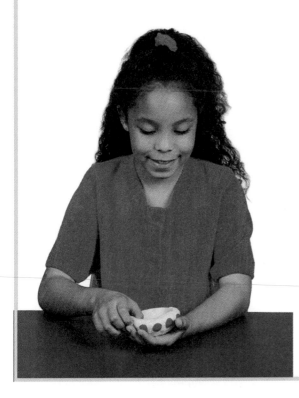

Think and Do

Make a pot from clay. Work the clay into a shape. Try using different colors of clay to make your pot more interesting.

Tell What You Know

1. Tell how matter is being changed in each picture.

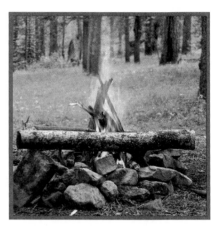

Vocabulary

Tell which pictures answer the questions.

2. Which picture shows an *irreversible* change?

3. Which picture shows a *mixture*?

4. Which picture shows a *reversible* change?

a.

b.

c.

C52

Using Science Skills

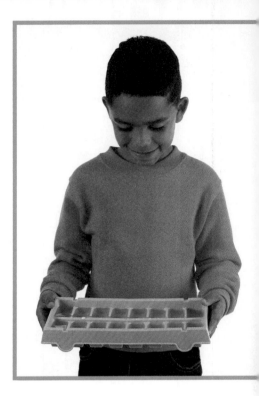

5. **Plan and Conduct a Simple Investigation/Predict** Plan a way to show how water can change from a liquid to a solid and back to a liquid. List the materials you will need. Draw pictures to show each step you will take. Predict what will happen, and then follow your plan. Did you predict correctly?

6. **Observe/Classify** Look at pictures in magazines. Find three kinds of foods that are mixtures. Then make a chart like this one. Write the name of each mixture. Then list the foods that make up each one.

Food Mixtures		
Mixture 1	Mixture 2	Mixture 3
_____	_____	_____

The Strength of Air

1. Close a zip-top bag around a straw. Then blow into the straw.

2. Pull out the straw, and quickly finish zipping the bag closed.

3. How many books can you pile on your bag of air? Record what you observe.

4. Does air take up space? Can the air in the bag hold a lot of books? Share what you observe.

Disappearing Water

1. Pour the same amount of water into two clear cups that are the same size and shape.

2. Use tape to mark the level of water in each cup.

3. Cover one cup with plastic wrap.

4. Leave the cups side-by-side for a few days.

5. Write about what you observe. What happens to the water in the two cups? Why?

Weigh Some Objects

1. Use a carton, a rubber band, a paper clip, and string to make a hanging box.

2. Use a ruler to measure the length of the rubber band. Record the length.

3. Put a few small objects in the box. As you add each one, measure and record the rubber band's length.

4. Tell why the rubber band stretched as you added more objects.

Make a Bottle Thermometer

1. Put colored water and a straw in a plastic bottle, as you see here.

2. Tape a card to the straw.

3. Set the bottle in a cool place. Mark the card to show how high the water goes.

4. Set the bottle in a warm place. Mark the card again.

5. Talk about what you observed.

CHAPTER 3

Forces and Motion

Vocabulary

force
location
wind
gravity
motion

Did You Know?
Cheetahs use **motion** to catch their food. They are the fastest land animals.

The force that pulls things toward the center of Earth is called **gravity** . A sled moves down a hill because of gravity. Gravity keeps us on the ground.

Because of gravity, objects fall to the ground unless something holds them up. If you hold an object, you are keeping it from falling. If you let go of the object, it will drop to the ground.

■ **Why did the pompom fall to the ground?**

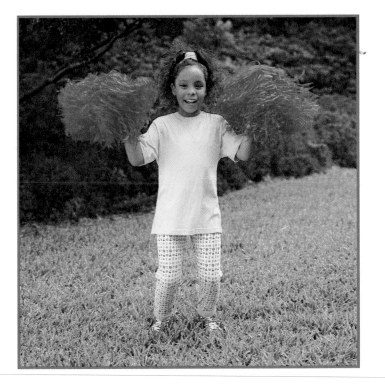

Magnetism

Magnetism is a force. A magnet attracts, or pulls on, objects made of some metals, such as iron. If you drop some iron nails, you can use a magnet to pick them up.

A magnet has a magnetic field. This is the space where the magnet's force acts. A magnet pulls on an iron object in its magnetic field even without touching the object.

■ **Why is the magnet pulling up these iron nails?**

A magnet can attract an iron object through certain other materials, including plastic, paper, water, and glass. If the material is too thick, the magnet will not attract the iron object.

■ **What force is the child using to make the picture?**

Think About It

1. What is a force?
2. How can you use forces?

How Can We Measure Motion?

One Way to Measure Motion

You will need

board

6 books

meterstick

toy truck

1 Make a low ramp. Let the toy truck roll down.

2 Measure from the bottom of the ramp to where the truck stopped. Record the distance.

3 Make the ramp higher. Then repeat Steps 1 and 2.

4 Use numbers to compare your data. When did the truck go farther? Why?

Science Skill
You can use numbers to find out how far an object moves.

Measuring Motion

Forces can make people and things move. When something moves, it is in **motion**. These people are in motion. What force is making them move?

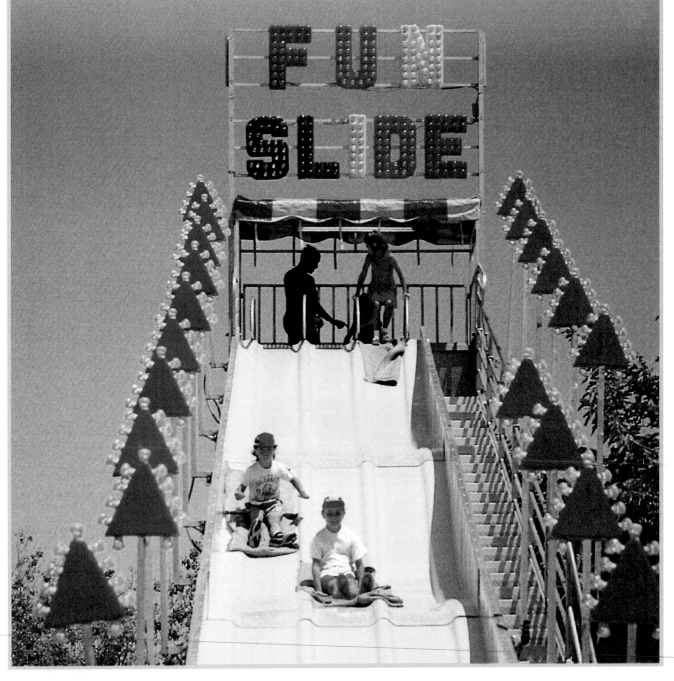

Force and Motion

Something light is easier to move than something heavy. Less force is needed to move light things, and more force is needed to move heavy things.

It also takes less force to move something on a smooth surface than on a rough surface. It takes less force to pull a wagon on a sidewalk than on grass. A rough surface like grass causes more friction. Friction is a force that makes it harder to move things.

It takes less force to move something a short distance than a long distance. To move a ball a short distance, you kick it gently. To move it farther, you kick it hard.

■ **In which picture will the ball go farther? Why?**

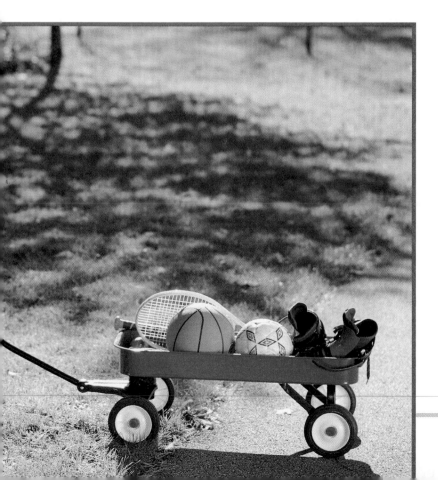

Ways to Measure Motion

You can measure how far something or someone moves. In a jumping contest, you try to jump as far as you can. Someone measures how far you jump.

■ **What tool is being used to measure how far the girl jumps?**

You can also measure how much time something or someone takes to move from one place to another. In a race, a timekeeper measures how much time racers take to reach the finish line.

02:47

You can use a rubber band to measure how much force it takes to move something. The rubber band stretches less when you pull with less force. It stretches more when you pull with more force.

■ **Which picture shows more force being used?**

Think About It

1. What makes things move?

2. How can you measure motion?

Math/Literature Link

The Enormous Turnip

The folktale *The Enormous Turnip* is about a turnip so big that a man cannot pull it up. How will the man and his family pull up the turnip? You can read the book to find out how much force it takes.

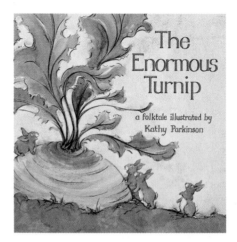

Think and Do

See how much force it takes to move things. Tie a book to a spring scale. Pull on the spring scale. As the book moves, read the numbers on the scale. Repeat with other objects, and compare the numbers. Which object needs the most force to be moved?

A Personal Trainer

A personal trainer teaches people how to exercise the right way. This personal trainer is showing a woman how to use a weight machine. The bar of this machine connects to weights. The woman must pull down and push up on the bar to move the weights.

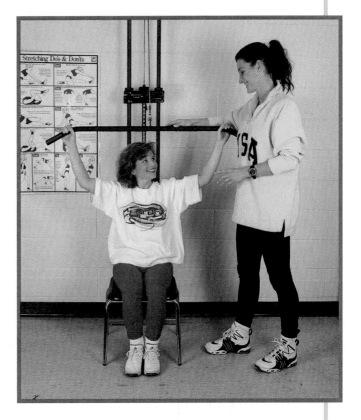

Think and Do

Think of some exercises you know how to do. As you do each one, observe when you are pushing or pulling. Then show a classmate how to do the exercises. Use the words *push* and *pull.*

Tell What You Know

Tell which picture answers each question.

a.　　b.　　c.　　d.　　e.

1. How can gravity change an object's location?

2. How can you measure how far a thing moves?

3. How can you measure how long someone takes to move from one place to another?

4. How can a push change an object's direction?

5. Which is a pull?

Vocabulary

6. Use these words to tell about the picture.

force	location
gravity	motion

Using Science Skills

7. Observe Make a chart like this one, and then observe objects in motion. What force moves each object? Write whether the force is a *push* or a *pull*.

Which Forces Move Objects?				
Object	Wind	Water	Gravity	Magnet
Boat	push	push		

8. Use Numbers Make a ramp like this one. Place a toy car at the top, and let it go. Measure how far the car travels. Then cover the ramp with a thick towel and try again. When does the car travel farther? faster?

Try two other surfaces. Use numbers to measure each distance, and compare.

CHAPTER **4**

Sound

Vocabulary

sound
vibrate
loudness
pitch
sonar
music

Did You Know?

Elephants can make and hear sounds that are so low in **pitch** that humans can't hear them.

Did You Know?
Crickets hear **sound** through ears on their legs.

ear

LESSON 1

What Is Sound?

Investigate

What Makes Sound

You will need

ruler

paper and pencil

1 Hold the ruler on a desk so one end hangs over the edge. Push that end down and let it go.

2 Observe and record what happens.

3 How could you change the sound? Plan an investigation.

4 Follow your plan. Tell a classmate what you find out.

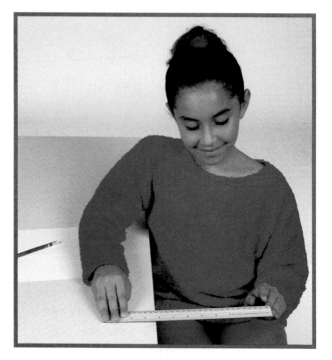

Science Skill
When you plan an investigation, you ask a question and test ways to answer the question.

C78

What Makes Sound

The energy that lets you hear is **sound**. Sound is made when things **vibrate**, or move back and forth very fast.

Sound and Air

When something vibrates, it makes the air around it vibrate, too. The strings of a guitar vibrate when you pluck them. The vibrations travel through the air to your ears. Then you hear the sound the guitar makes.

Sound moves through the air in every direction. When a school bell rings, people all around the bell can hear it.

Sound can also be blocked. Some people who work near loud machines wear ear coverings. The coverings block some of the sound vibrations from reaching their ears.

■ **Why did this person cover his ears?**

How You Hear Sounds

You hear sounds with your ears. Sound vibrations move through the air into each ear. The vibrations reach your eardrum and make it vibrate.

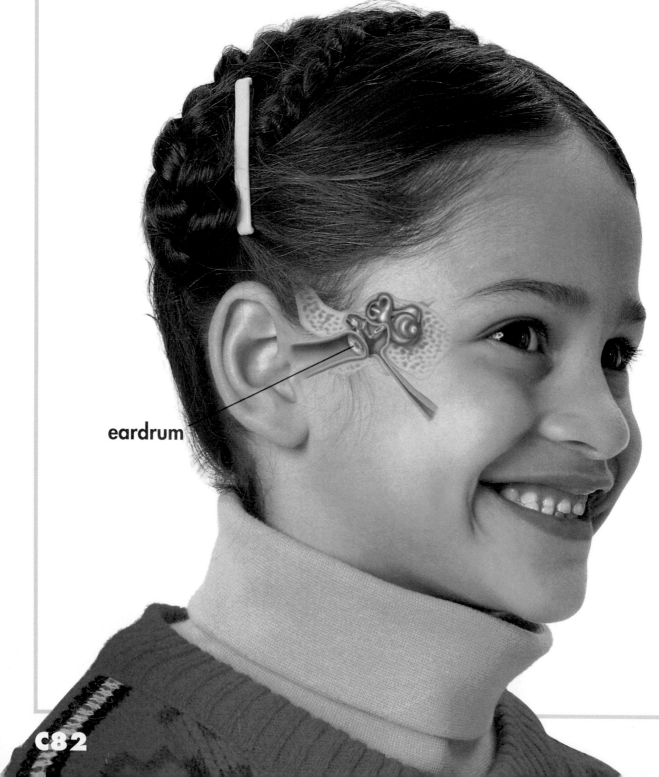

eardrum

How You Make Sounds

You use your vocal cords to make sounds in your throat. Put your hand on your throat when you talk, and you can feel the vocal cords vibrate.

Audiologist

An audiologist tests people's hearing with machines that make sounds. An audiologist also helps people who do not hear well. You should get your hearing checked by an audiologist from time to time.

■ **What is this audiologist doing?**

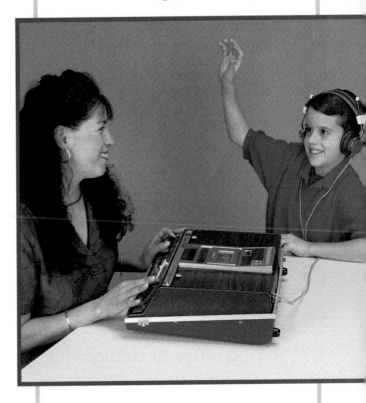

Think About It

1. What makes sound?
2. How do you hear sounds?

How Do Sounds Vary?

Different Sounds

You will need

3 glasses

water

spoon

paper and pencil

1 Pour a different amount of water into each glass.

2 Tap the side of each glass with the spoon.

3 Listen to the sounds. Record what you observe.

4 Find ways to change the sounds. Observe and record.

Science Skill
Listening is one way to observe.

How Sounds Can Be Different

Sounds are all around you. What sounds do you think the children in the picture hear? What sounds can you hear in your classroom?

Loud and Soft

Sounds are different in **loudness**, or how loud or soft they are. Some sounds, like yells, are loud. Other sounds, like whispers, are soft. It takes less energy to make a soft sound than a loud sound.

■ What do you do to make a loud sound?

High and Low

Sounds are also different in **pitch**, or how high or low they are. A sparrow's song is a high sound. A bullfrog's croak is a low sound.

■ How are the sounds a sparrow and a bullfrog make different?

Think About It

1. What are some loud sounds and some soft sounds?
2. What are some high sounds and some low sounds?

How Does Sound Travel?

How Sound Travels

You will need

meterstick   tape   paper and pencil

1 Measure 50 centimeters on your desk. Mark each end with tape.

2 Sit next to one tape mark, and scratch the other one. Record what you hear.

3 Predict the loudness of the sound if you put your ear on the desk. Record what you predict.

4 Try it. What do you observe? Did you predict correctly?

Science Skill

To predict, think about what you already know and then say what you think will happen.

How Sound Travels

Sound can travel through different kinds of matter. These children have their ears under water. They can still hear the coach's voice. What kinds of matter are the sounds traveling through?

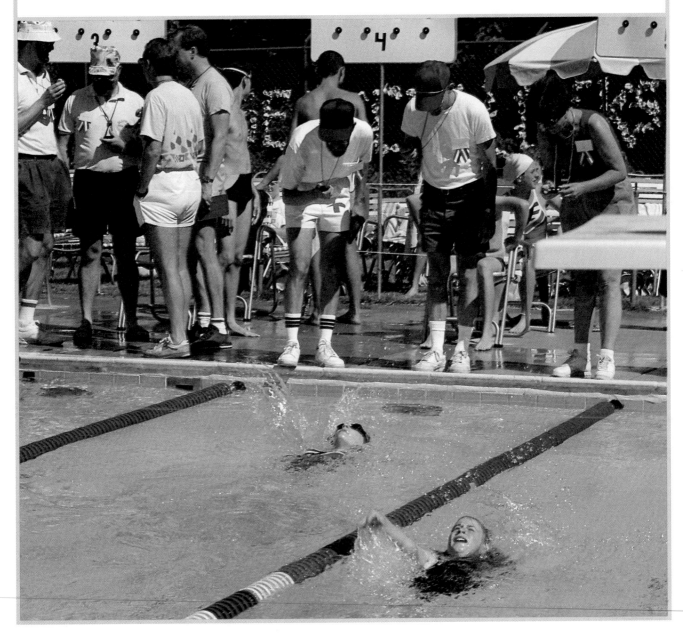

Sounds Travel Through Gases and Solids

Sounds can travel through gases such as air. The sound from the vibrating bells that are on some alarm clocks travels through the air. It reaches a person's ears and wakes the person up.

■ **What does the sound from the horn travel through?**

Sounds can also travel through solid objects. You may have played with a string telephone. A person talks into one cup, making the air inside it vibrate. The air makes the cup vibrate, and the cup makes the string vibrate.

The vibrations travel through the string and make the other cup vibrate. That cup makes the air inside it vibrate. The vibrations travel into the other person's ear, and that person hears the sound.

■ **What vibrates when a person talks into the cup?**

Sound Travels Through Liquids

Sounds can travel through liquids, such as water. Dolphins have a kind of **sonar**, or a way to use sounds to locate objects under water. The sounds make echoes when they hit objects. The dolphins locate the objects by listening to the echoes.

dolphins

Humpback whales also make sounds under water. The sounds they make are like songs. The songs can travel a long way through the water to other whales.

■ **What do you think this whale is communicating to her young?**

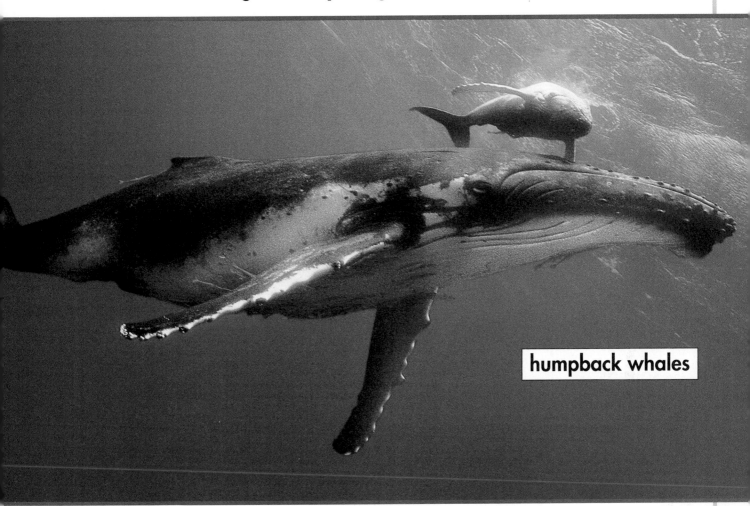

humpback whales

Think About It

1. How do sounds travel?

2. What can sounds travel through?

How Can We Make Different Sounds?

Investigate

Making Different Sounds

You will need

rubber bands

box lid

pencil

1. Stretch 3 rubber bands around the box lid.

2. Pluck the rubber bands. Compare the sounds.

3. Put the pencil under the rubber bands and pluck them again. Compare.

4. How did the sounds change? How did they stay the same?

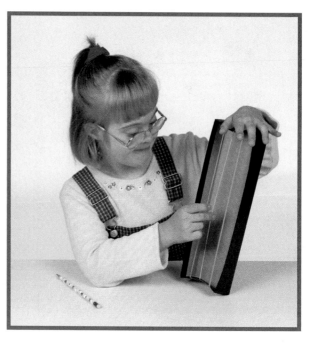

Science Skill

When you compare, you look for ways that two or more things are alike and different.

How to Make Different Sounds

People use sounds to make **music**, or a combination of sounds that people enjoy. These people are playing different musical instruments. Each instrument makes a different kind of sound.

Making Different Sounds

Some musical instruments have strings. Thin strings vibrate faster and make higher sounds. Thick strings vibrate more slowly and make lower sounds.

Changing the length of a string changes how fast it vibrates. Shortening a string makes it vibrate faster and sound higher. Making the string longer makes it vibrate more slowly and sound lower.

You can change the loudness of a sound. If you use a lot of energy and hit a drum hard, it makes a loud sound. If you use just a little energy and tap the drum lightly, it makes a soft sound.

■ **How can you make different sounds with these instruments?**

Think About It

1. How can you make high sounds and low sounds?
2. How can you make loud sounds and soft sounds?

Math Link

How Long Does a Sound Last?

This musical instrument is called a triangle. When a player taps the triangle, it makes a ringing sound.

Think and Do

Tap a triangle gently. Count slowly to time how long you can hear the sound. Then hit the triangle harder. Count at the same speed to time how long you can hear this sound.

Which sound lasts longer? Write a subtraction problem to show how much longer it lasted.

Make Musical Instruments

Musical instruments can be grouped by the way they make sounds. Percussion instruments make sounds when you shake or hit them. Stringed instruments make sounds when you pluck their strings. Wind instruments make sounds when you blow into them.

percussion   stringed   wind

Think and Do

Make a musical instrument of your own. Then show a classmate how it works. Tell if it is a wind, a stringed, or a percussion instrument.

Tell What You Know

Answer the question about each picture.

1. What vibrates to make the sound?

2. How can you change this sound?

3. How are these sounds different?

Vocabulary

Use each word to tell about a picture.

4. sonar

5. music

6. pitch

a.

b.

c.

Using Science Skills

7. **Observe/Compare** Make a chart like this one. Then listen for different sounds. Write the information in your chart.

Kinds of Sounds		
Sound Maker	High or Low	Loud or Soft

8. **Plan an Investigation/Compare** Investigate how to change the pitch of a sound. Blow into a bottle filled with water. Listen to the sound. Now think of ways to change its pitch. Try out your ideas.

Activities
for Home or School

Push or Pull Toys?

1. Observe some toys. Do you push them or pull them or both?

2. Make a chart to classify the toys as toys you push, toys you pull, or both.

3. Use your chart to help you communicate to classmates what you observe.

Magnetic Puppet Show

1. Draw puppets on cardboard. Cut them out.

2. Bend the bottom of the puppet back to make a tab. Tape a paper clip onto the tab.

3. Cut off one side of a box to make a stage.

4. Place the puppets on the stage.

5. Use magnets under the stage to move the puppets around.

C102

Make Chicken Sounds

1. Punch two holes in the bottom of a paper cup.

2. Push a string through the holes and tie a knot.

3. Wet the string. Move your fingers along the string in short, jerky movements.

4. Tell what sounds you hear and how they are made.

Play a Listening Game

1. All players but the one who is "it" close their eyes.

2. The player who is "it" makes a sound.

3. The other players guess how the sound is being made. They may need clues from the player who is "it."

4. The first player to guess correctly makes the next sound.

WRITING

Sound Off Write an announcement about something happening at school. Make a paper megaphone or another tool to share your message.

READING

Puddle Jumper: How a Toy Is Made
by Ann Morris
How does a toymaker change matter to make a moving toy? Talk about what you learn.

COMPUTER CENTER
Visit *The Learning Site* at www.harcourtschool.com/ca

Extension Chapters

California Science Standards

Extension Chapters

California Science Standards

CHAPTER 1

The Sun, the Moon, and Stars

Vocabulary

sun
energy
solar energy
rotation
orbit
season
moon
moonlight
crater
constellation

Did You Know?

The **sun** is so large that more than a million Earths could fit inside it.

Did You Know?

The **moon** has no air or water, and the sky is always black.

What Causes Day and Night?

Where the Sun Is

You will need

paper and pencil

Where the Sun Is			
	Day 1	Day 2	Day 3
10:00 a.m.			
2:00 p.m.			

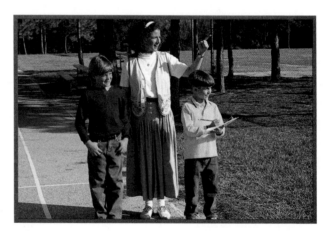

1 Observe where the sun is in the morning. Record.

 CAUTION Never look directly at the sun.

2 From the same place, observe where the sun is in the afternoon. Record.

3 Observe the sun at the same times for 2 more days. Record.

4 What pattern do you see?

Science Skill

A pattern of something happening over and over at the same place and time is a time/space relationship.

Day and Night

Each day, the sun seems to move across the sky. The sun does not really cross our sky. It is Earth that is moving. Because Earth moves, we have day and night.

sunrise

noon

sunset

The Sun

The **sun** is the star closest to Earth. The sun is much larger than Earth. It looks small only because it is far away.

The sun is made of hot gases. The gases are so hot, they give off light and heat. Light and heat are kinds of **energy** because they can cause change and do work.

sun

Most living things on Earth use **solar energy**, or light and heat from the sun. Plants use the sun's light to make food. Animals and people use its light to see in the daytime. The sun's heat warms water, land, air, and all living things on Earth.

■ **What does the sun look like here?**

Earth's Rotation

Earth is shaped something like a sphere, or a ball. It spins round and round in space. The spinning of Earth is called its **rotation**. It takes about 24 hours for Earth to rotate, or spin, all the way around one time. One full rotation of Earth is one full day.

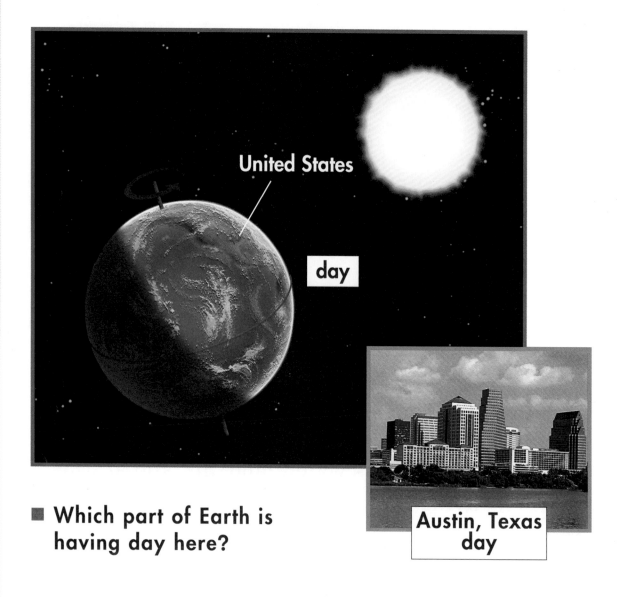

United States

day

Austin, Texas
day

■ Which part of Earth is having day here?

The sun shines all the time, but not always on your part of Earth. Earth's rotation causes each part of Earth to have light and dark each day.

When one side of Earth faces the sun, that side is lighted, and it is daytime. The other side of Earth is dark, and it is nighttime.

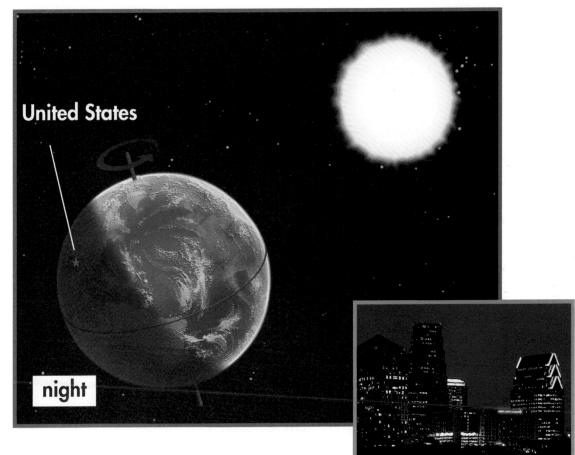

United States

night

Austin, Texas
night

Think About It

1. What is the sun?
2. Why does Earth have day and night?

What Causes the Seasons?

How Sunlight Shines on Earth

You will need

ball with
pencil

lamp

1 Tilt the ball so the top
of the pencil points
toward the light.

2 Where is the light the
brightest? Record.

3 Move the ball to the other side of the light.
Keep the tilt of the pencil the same. See the
picture above.

4 Observe where the light is the
brightest now. Record and discuss.

Science Skill
To observe light here,
you need only your
sense of sight.

What Causes the Seasons

Earth rotates on an imaginary line called an axis. Earth tilts on this axis. At the same time, Earth moves around the sun. For these reasons, Earth has different seasons.

North America

light from the sun

South America

Earth Orbits the Sun

Earth moves in an **orbit**, or a path, around the sun. It takes Earth one year to orbit the sun. As Earth orbits the sun, the seasons change. A **season** is a time of the year that has a certain kind of weather.

Earth

fall

sun

winter

summer

spring

Why the Seasons Change

Earth is always tilted in the same direction. When Earth is on one side of the sun, part of Earth faces the sun directly and gets more direct sunlight. This part of Earth has summer.

■ **Is the tilt of Earth the same or different in spring and summer?**

spring

summer

When Earth moves to the other side of the sun, Earth still tilts in the same direction. Now the tilt causes this same part of Earth to face the sun on a slant. Sunlight does not hit Earth as directly. This part of Earth has winter.

Think About It

1. How does Earth move around the sun?
2. Why do the seasons change?

fall

winter

How Does the Moon Move and Change?

Investigate

Light from the Moon

You will need

foam ball   foil   pencil   flashlight

1. With a partner, cover the ball with foil. Push the pencil into it to make a handle.

2. Observe how the ball looks in the dark. Draw it.

3. Hold the ball by the handle. Have your partner shine the flashlight on the ball. Draw and compare.

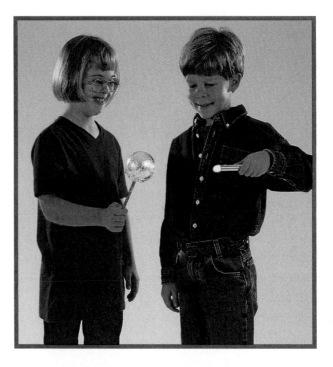

Science Skill
When you compare, you tell how two things are alike and different.

Moonlight

The **moon** is the largest object you can see in the night sky. It seems to shine, but the moon does not really give off its own light. The light from the moon, or **moonlight**, comes from the sun.

moon

The Moon

The moon is a huge ball of rock that orbits Earth. It takes about 29 days for the moon to orbit Earth.

When we look at the moon, it seems to have spots. Some spots are holes called craters. A **crater** is made when a large rock moving through space hits the moon.

■ **Which part of the moon is lighted by the sun?**

Earth

moon

sun

crater

Astronauts explore space and have gone to the moon. They have seen the craters and the gray dust that covers the moon. They have brought moon rocks back to Earth. Astronaut David Scott commanded the *Apollo 15* mission to the moon.

■ **What do you think this astronaut saw?**

The Moon Seems to Change Shape

The moon's orbit makes the moon seem to change shape. At the start of the moon's orbit, the moon is between the sun and Earth. The sun shines directly on the part of the moon that faces it. We cannot see this new moon from Earth.

In one week, the moon is one-fourth, or one-quarter, of the way through its orbit. From Earth the moon looks like a half-circle.

In two weeks, the moon is halfway around its orbit. Now Earth is between the sun and the moon. From Earth the moon looks like a full circle.

In three weeks, the moon is three-fourths of the way around. In four weeks, the moon is back where it started.

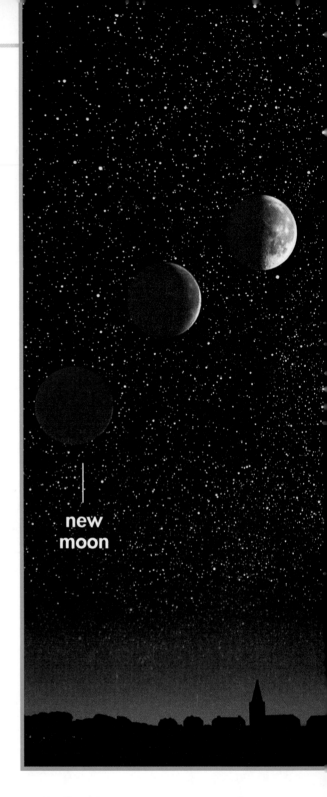

new moon

■ Why can't we see the new moon?

full
moon

quarter
moon

Think About It

1. What makes the moon seem to shine?

2. Why does the moon seem to change shape?

What Can We See in the Night Sky?

Investigate

Star Pictures

You will need

"star" cups

flashlight

black paper

tape

1. Tape the paper to a wall, and choose a star cup.

2. Point the bottom of the cup toward the paper.

3. Shine the flashlight through the cup. What do you see? Record.

4. Repeat with the other cups. Communicate to classmates what you observe.

Science Skill

When you communicate, you tell others what you think through writing, drawing, or speaking.

The Night Sky

On a clear night, you can see many stars. They look like small points of light in the night sky. Stars are really much bigger than Earth. They look small because they are far away.

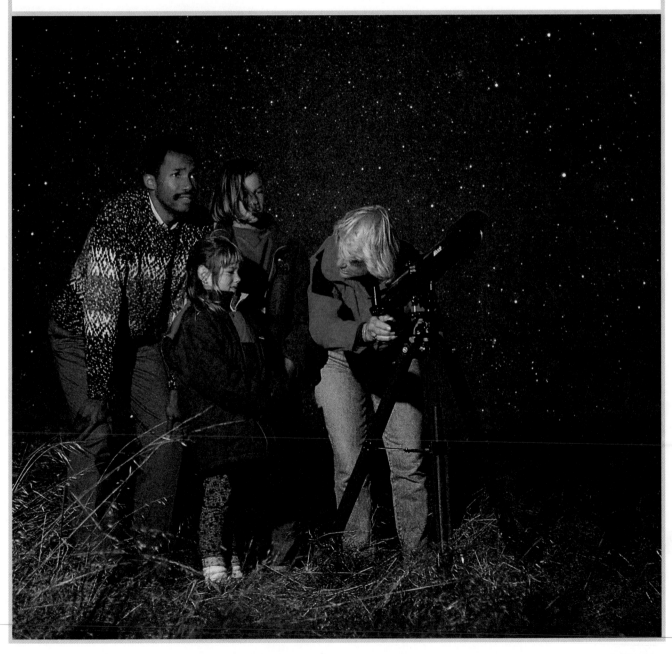

Stars and Planets

Stars are big balls of hot gases. The hot gases give off light. This light is what we see from Earth. Stars may appear to twinkle.

Some stars seem brighter than others. They may look brighter because they are bigger or hotter. They may also look brighter because they are closer to Earth.

■ **What else might you see in the night sky?**

comet

Milky Way

planet Mars

You may also see planets in the night sky. Planets may look larger and brighter than stars, and they do not twinkle. They do not give off their own light, as stars do.

Some people use telescopes to look at the night sky. A telescope makes things look closer and larger.

■ **How might stars look through a telescope?**

E25

Constellations

Long ago, people saw groups of stars that seemed to form pictures. They named the different star pictures. A group of stars that form a star picture is called a **constellation** .

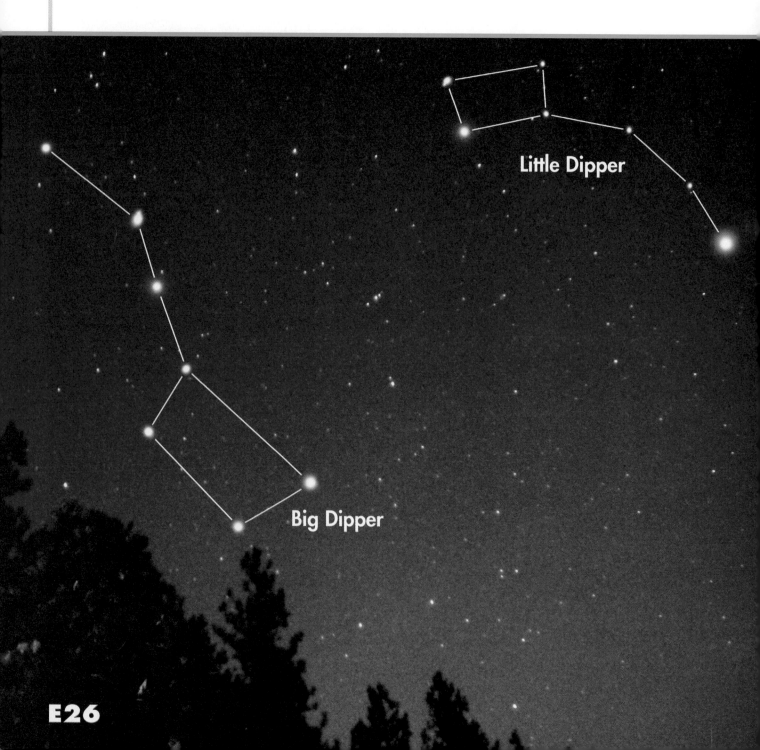

Little Dipper

Big Dipper

Using Science Skills

6. **Compare** Think about summer and winter where you live. Is it warmer in summer or in winter? Are there more hours of daylight in summer or in winter? How do you know?

Write three sentences that compare summer and winter. You may draw pictures, too.

7. **Use Time/Space Relationship** The moon orbits Earth in about 29 days. As the moon moves, it seems to change shape. Choose three pictures of the moon from pages E20 and E21. For each one, draw a picture to show where the sun, the moon, and Earth are when the moon looks that way.

Trace Your Shadow

1. On a sunny morning, ask a partner to use chalk to trace your shadow on a sidewalk.

2. Write the time of day on your shadow, and predict how your shadow will look later in the day.

3. In the afternoon, trace a new shadow. Compare.

Observe the Night Sky

1. With an adult, go outside on a clear night.

2. Find the moon. What shape is it?

3. Draw pictures of what you observe.

4. Do the activity again in one week.

5. Communicate how your pictures are different and why.

Which Paper Towel Dries First?

1. With a family member or a classmate, wet three paper towels.

2. Put each towel in a different place.

3. Predict which towel will dry first.

4. Check the towels every 15 minutes. Which one dries first? last? Why?

Make Sun Prints

1. Cut two shapes from construction paper.

2. Place the shapes on black paper.

3. With an adult, go outside. Leave one sheet of black paper in the shade and the other one in the sun.

4. After several hours, remove the cutouts from the black paper. Observe. Why do you think this happens?

Changes in Habitats

Vocabulary

drought
pollution
litter
reuse
recycle

Did You Know?

If you **recycle** a stack of newspapers that is 4 feet tall, you will keep one tree from being cut down.

Did You Know?

Plants help clean up air **pollution** as they take in air.

How Does Weather Change Habitats?

Weather and Seeds

You will need

seeds

2 paper plates

4 wet paper towels

spray bottle

paper and pencil

1 Lay a wet towel on each plate. Put 4 seeds on each towel. Cover with another wet towel.

2 Put the plates in a warm place. Keep the towels on one plate wet.

3 Check the seeds each day. Record what you observe.

4 Draw a conclusion about whether seeds outdoors need rain.

Science Skill
Use your observations and what you know to draw a conclusion.

How Rain Changes the Land

Plants and animals need certain things. Sometimes too little or too much rain changes their habitats. Then plants and animals may not have what they need.

dry wheat fields

Droughts

A pond can dry up when there is no rain for a long time. A long time without rain is called a **drought**. Without enough water, most pond plants die. Many pond animals move to other ponds.

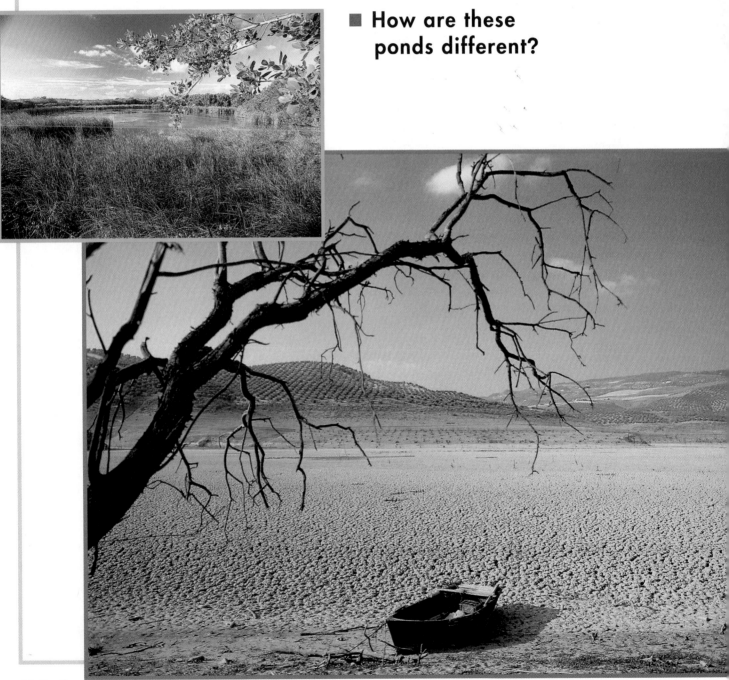

■ **How are these ponds different?**

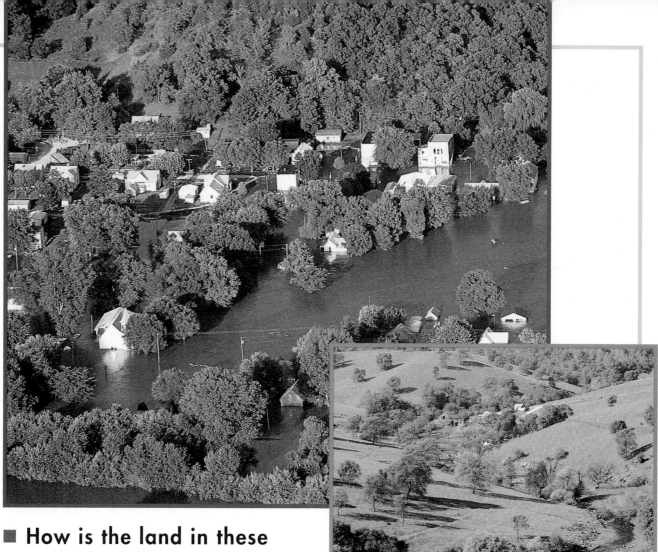

■ **How is the land in these pictures different?**

Floods

When it rains for a long time, rainwater may flood the land. Then the plants and animals get too much water. Plants die and animals move to drier places.

Lightning and Fire

Sometimes lightning strikes a tree in a forest. If the forest is dry, the tree may catch fire. The fire may burn other trees and spread through the forest.

Some animals may die. Other animals may be able to move quickly to safer places.

After a fire burns a forest, some seeds begin to germinate. Birds drop other seeds on the ground. The seeds grow into new plants, and many animals come back. Over time, the forest begins to look the way it did before the fire.

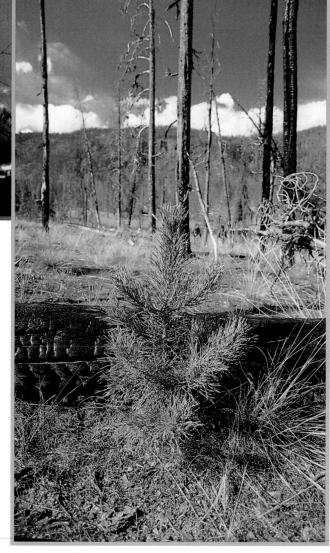

■ **What conclusion can you draw from this picture?**

Think About It

1. How can too little rain or too much rain change an environment?
2. How does a fire change an environment?

How Does Pollution Change Environments?

Whether Soil and Sand Can Clean Water

You will need

sand

soil

coffee filter

funnel

container

Colored Water

colored water

1 Put the funnel and then the filter in the container, as shown. Add sand and then soil to make a natural filter.

2 Pour the colored water into your sand-and-soil filter. What do you observe?

3 Your filter works the way the soil outside does. Does the sand-and-soil filter clean the colored water?

Science Skill

When you observe, you use your senses to learn what happens.

How Pollution Changes an Environment

Waste that harms land, water, or air is called **pollution**. Pollution also harms the plants and animals that use the land, water, and air.

Land Pollution

When people put trash in a trash can, the trash may be put in a landfill. Trash that is not put in a trash can is called **litter**. Litter hurts plants and animals. It covers up plants so they cannot get light. Animals may eat litter and get sick.

■ **How has this garbage dump changed the land?**

Air Pollution

Plants and animals need clean air. Air gets dirty, or polluted, when some factories and cars put out smoke and fumes. This air pollution can make plants and animals sick.

■ **What is polluting the air?**

Water Pollution

All living things need clean water. Water pollution changes rivers, lakes, and streams. Waste from factories and other places can harm plants and animals.

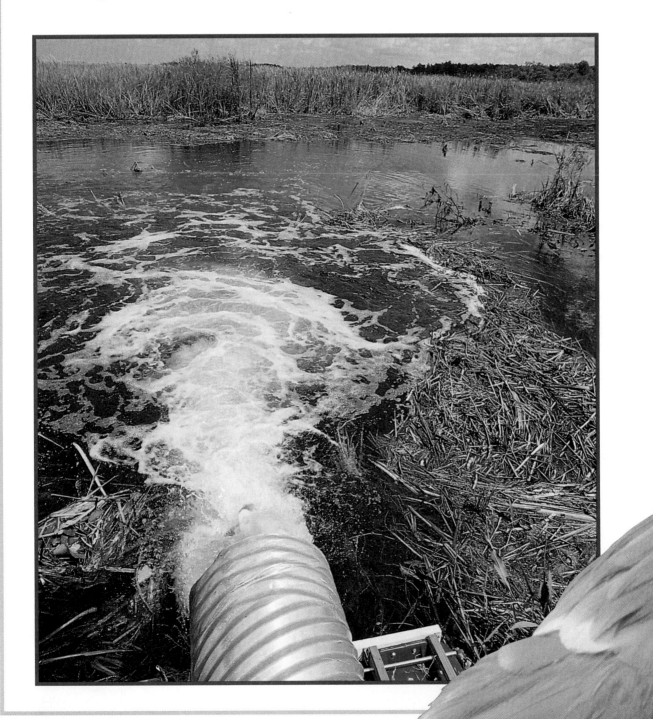

Litter thrown into water is another kind of pollution that hurts animals. If animals eat litter, they may get sick. Litter also gets caught around animals' bodies. Then the animals have trouble moving and eating.

■ **How is litter harming this bird?**

Think About It

1. What are some kinds of pollution?
2. How does pollution harm plants and animals?

How Do People Help the Environment?

How Things Can Be Reused

You will need

used things

markers or paint

glue

newspaper

1 Observe the used things. Could you use them to make something new?

2 List the steps you plan to take. Follow your plan.

3 Use your plan to communicate to a classmate how you made something new.

Science Skill

When you list the steps you plan to take, you make it easier to communicate them.

Ways People Help the Environment

People can take care of their environment and keep it clean. They can pick up litter and make less trash. How are these people helping the environment?

E49

Taking Care of the Land

Some people plant trees. These trees may become new homes for animals. The roots of the trees hold the soil so it will not blow away or wash away.

People take care of the land when they put litter in trash cans. In many places, people work together to pick up litter.

■ **How are these people taking care of the land?**

Making less trash is another way people can take care of the land. People decided to **reuse**, or use again, old tires to build this playground.

People also make less trash by recycling. To **recycle** means to use old materials to make new things. Metal cans and plastic bottles may be melted down to make other things.

Taking Care of the Air

People can take care of the air by making less pollution. People sometimes choose to walk or ride bicycles instead of driving their cars everywhere. Many factories have found ways to put less pollution in the air.

■ **What is this person doing to help keep the air clean?**

Taking Care of the Water

People can help keep water clean in rivers, lakes, streams, and oceans. Some people help by picking up litter. Many factory owners are finding ways for their factories to get rid of waste without putting it into the water.

■ **How are these people helping take care of the water?**

Think About It

1. How can people keep the environment clean?
2. What are some ways people can make less pollution?

How Much Paper Trash Could You Reuse?

A landfill has many kinds of trash. It may have old bottles, empty cans, and even broken television sets. Paper is what takes up the most space in a landfill.

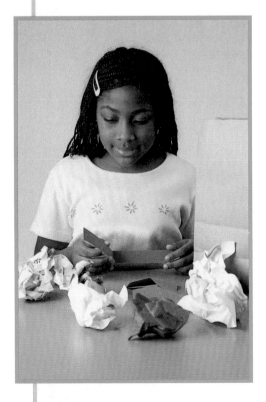

Think and Do

Keep a large bag at the front of the classroom for one day. Throw all your paper trash in it.

At the end of the day, count the papers you could reuse. Then count the papers you could not reuse. Compare. Are there more papers you could reuse or more papers you could not reuse?

Archaeologists Investigate Trash

Long ago, many people threw their trash into holes in the ground. Today archaeologists dig up the trash in these holes. Archaeologists are scientists who study how people lived long ago.

The trash helps them learn more about the people who threw it away. A broken toy may show that a family had a child. A jar may show what people liked to eat.

 Think and Do

Check your classroom trash and make a chart like this one. Write what each piece of trash tells about your class.

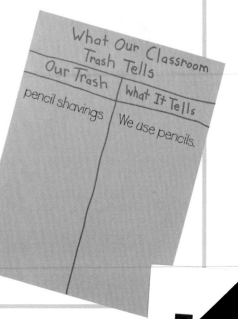

What Our Classroom Trash Tells

Our Trash	What It Tells
pencil shavings	We use pencils.

Tell What You Know

Tell what you know about each picture.

1. **2.** **3.** **4.**

Vocabulary

Match each word with a
picture that shows its
meaning.

5. pollution

6. recycle

7. litter

8. reuse

a. **b.**

c. **d.**

Using Science Skills

9. Draw Conclusions These two pictures show the same lake.

before

after

What conclusion can you draw about what happened to the lake?

10. Compare What things do your school and your neighborhood recycle? Make a chart like this one. Compare the things you see being recycled at school and in your neighborhood.

Things I See Recycled		
Objects	School	Neighborhood
Glass Bottles		卌
Paper	卌 ||	||

Recycle and Reuse

Make a recycling chart.
Show the kinds of
things that can be
recycled or reused.

See What Is in the Air

1. Spread petroleum jelly on the center of an index card.

2. Place the card outdoors on a windowsill.

3. The next day observe the card with a hand lens.

4. Draw and write about what you see.

5. Put another card in a different place. Do the activity again. Compare what happens.

References

Investigating

This plan will help you work like a scientist.

STEP 1 — Ask a question.

Which paper towel will be the strongest when wet?

STEP 2 — Make a prediction.

I predict this paper towel will be the strongest.

STEP 3 — Plan a fair test.

I will put each paper towel in water. Then I will put the same block on each towel to test it.

STEP 4 — Do your test.

I'll record what happens to each towel.

STEP 5 — Draw a conclusion.

My prediction was correct! This paper towel was the strongest.

Investigate More

Which paper towel will hold the most water?

Using Science Tools

Hand Lens

A hand lens makes things look larger than they are.

1. Hold the hand lens close to your face.
2. Move the object until you see it clearly.

Thermometer

Scientists use the Celsius scale on a thermometer to measure temperature.

1. Place the thermometer in the liquid.
2. Wait about two minutes.
3. Find the line that meets the top of the liquid.
4. Read the number. This is the temperature.

The temperature is 40°C.

This leaf is 21 centimeters long.

Ruler

A ruler is a tool that lets you measure how long something is.

1. Put the beginning edge of the ruler at the beginning point of the object.
2. Read the number at the other end.

Meterstick

A meterstick is a tool that lets you measure in centimeters.

1. Put the beginning edge of the meterstick at the beginning point.
2. Read the number at the other end to measure the distance.

This paper is 30 centimeters long.

Measuring Cup

Use a measuring cup to measure how much liquid there is.

1. Pour the liquid into the cup.
2. Put the cup on a table.
3. Wait until the liquid is still.
4. Look at the level of the liquid.
5. Read how much liquid is in the cup.

The cup has 350 milliliters of liquid in it.

Clock

A clock lets you measure time. Some clocks have a minute hand and an hour hand.

1. Look at the hour hand.
2. Look at the minute hand.
3. Read the time.

It is 11:30.

Stopwatch

Twenty-five seconds have gone by.

A stopwatch measures how much time passes.

1. To start timing, press START.
2. To stop timing, press STOP.
3. Read how much time has passed.

Balance

Use a balance to measure the mass of an object.

1. Make the pans even.
2. Put the object in one pan.
3. Add masses to the other pan until the pans are even again.
4. Count up the number of masses. The total is the mass of the object.

Computer

Computers are tools, too. Here are some ways a computer can help you.

1. Some computers help you draw or make charts.
2. Most computers help you find answers to questions.
3. Many computers help you communicate. This can mean writing, sending, or receiving information.

Measurements

1 cm

centimeter (cm) ruler

1 in.

inch (in.) ruler

Water freezes at 32°F. — Water freezes at 0°C.

Fahrenheit (F)
temperature

Celsius (C)
temperature

1 kilogram (kg)

1 pound (lb)

1 liter (L)

1 cup (c)

Health Handbook

Getting Exercise

Warm-Up and Cool-Down Stretches

▼ **Shoulder and Chest Stretch** Pull your hands slowly toward the floor. Keep your elbows straight, but don't lock them.

Warm up your muscles before you exercise. Spend at least five minutes stretching. You can use any of the stretches shown here. Hold each stretch while you count to 15. Repeat each stretch three times. Remember to start exercising slowly.

Slow down at the end of exercise. Then repeat some of these stretches for about two minutes. Stretching after exercise helps your muscles cool down.

▶ **Sit-and-Reach Stretch** Bend forward at the waist. Keep your eyes on your toes.

◀ **Calf Stretch** Keep both feet on the floor. Try changing the distance between your feet. Where do you get a better stretch?

R12

▲ **Upper Back and Shoulder Stretch**
Try to stretch your hand down so
that it rests flat against your back.

▼ **Thigh Stretch** Keep both hands
flat on the ground. Lean as far
forward as you can.

▲ **Leg Stretch**
Extend one leg
behind you. Keep
the toes of that
foot pointed up.

Tips for Stretching

- Never bounce. Stretch gently.
- Breathe normally to get the air you need.
- Never stretch until it hurts. You should
  feel only a slight pull.

Getting Exercise

Build Your Heart and Lungs

Exercise helps your heart and lungs grow strong. The best exercise activities make you breathe deeply. They make your heart beat fast. You should try to exercise for at least twenty minutes at a time. Remember to warm up first and cool down at the end.

▲ **Swimming** If you are not a strong swimmer, use a kickboard to get a good workout. Remember to swim only when a lifeguard is present.

◄ **Skating** Always wear a helmet, elbow and knee pads, wrist guards, and gloves. Learn to skate, stop, and fall correctly.

▼ **Riding a Bike** When you ride your bike, your exercise really gets you somewhere! Follow bike safety rules, and always wear your helmet.

▶ **Walking** A fast walk can help build your heart and lungs. Wear shoes that support your feet. Walk with a friend for extra fun!

▶ **Jumping Rope** Jumping rope is good for your heart and your lungs. Always jump on a flat surface. Wear shoes that support your feet.

R15

Staying Safe

Fire Safety

You can stay safe from fires. Follow these safety rules.

- Never play with matches or lighters.
- Be careful around stoves, heaters, fireplaces, and grills.
- Don't use microwaves, irons, or toasters without an adult's help.
- Practice your family's fire safety plan.
- If there is a fire in your home, get out quickly. Drop to the floor and crawl if the room is filled with smoke. If a closed door feels hot, don't open it. Use another exit. Call 911 from outside your home.
- If your clothes catch on fire, use Stop, Drop, and Roll right away to put out the flames.

❶ **Stop** Don't run or wave your arms.

❷ **Drop** Lie down quickly. Cover your eyes with your hands.

❸ **Roll** Roll back and forth to put out the fire.

Stranger Danger

NO!

You can stay safe around strangers. Follow these rules.

- Never talk to strangers.
- Never go with a stranger, on foot or in a car.
- If you are home alone, do not open the door. Do not let telephone callers know you are alone.
- Never give your name, address, or phone number to anyone you don't know. (You may give this information to a 911 operator in an emergency.)
- If you are lost or need help, talk to a police officer, a guard, or a store clerk.
- If a stranger bothers you, use the Stranger Danger rules to stay safe.

❶ Say no! Yell if you need to. You do not have to be polite to strangers.

❷ Get away. Walk fast or run in the opposite direction. Go toward people who can help you.

❸ Tell someone. Tell a trusted adult, such as a family member, a teacher, or a police officer. Do not keep secrets about strangers.

Bike Safety
A Safe Bike

To ride your bike safely, you need to start with a safe bike. A safe bike is the right size for you. When you sit on your bike with the pedal in the lowest position, you should be able to rest your heel on the pedal.

After checking the size of your bike, check to see that it has the right safety equipment. Your bike should have everything shown below.

horn

white reflector

red reflector

clear reflector

clear reflector

reflectors

Your Bike Helmet

◄ Always wear a bike helmet. Wear your helmet flat on your head. Be sure it is strapped tightly. If your helmet gets bumped in a fall, replace it right away, even if it doesn't look damaged.

Safety on the Road

- Check your bike for safety every time you ride it.
- Ride in single file. Ride in the same direction as traffic.
- Stop, look, listen, and think when you enter a street or cross a driveway.
- Walk your bike across an intersection.
- Obey all traffic signs and signals.
- Don't ride at night without an adult. Wear light-colored clothing and use lights and reflectors for night riding.

Sense Organs

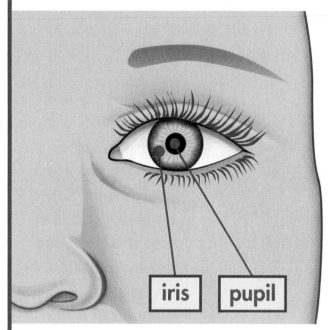

Outside of Eye

Caring for Your Eyes and Ears

- Sunglasses protect your eyes. Wear sunglasses when you are outdoors in sunlight or snow or on the water.
- Never put anything in your ears.

Eyes

Your eyes let you see. When you look at your eyes, you see a white part, a colored part, and a hole. The colored part is the iris. The hole in the middle is the pupil.

Inside of Eye

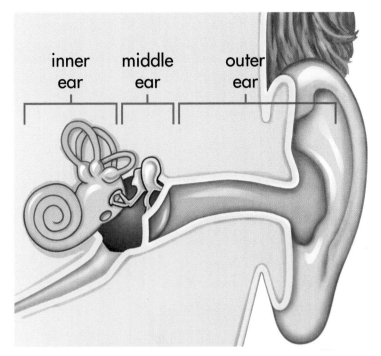

inner
ear   middle
ear   outer
ear

Inside of Ear   **Outside of Ear**

Ears

Your ears let you hear. What you see on the outside of your head is only part of your ear. The main part of your ear is inside your head.

ACTIVITIES

1. Put your hand over one eye for thirty seconds. Look in a mirror and take your hand away from your eye. What happens to the pupil of that eye?

2. Put on a blindfold and cover one ear. Ask a classmate to stand somewhere in the room and clap. Point to where the sound came from. Are you pointing in the right direction?

The Respiratory System

When you breathe, you are using your respiratory system. Your mouth, your nose, your lungs, and your diaphragm are parts of your respiratory system.

Caring for Your Respiratory System

- Never put anything in your nose.

- Playing helps your lungs. When you climb and jump, you breathe harder. Breathing harder makes your lungs stronger.

nose

mouth

lungs

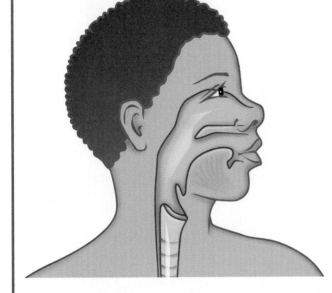

Mouth and Nose

Air goes in and out of your body through your mouth and nose. Your mouth and nose warm the air you breathe.

Lungs

You have two lungs. Your lungs are in your chest. When you breathe in, your lungs fill with air. When you breathe out, air leaves your lungs.

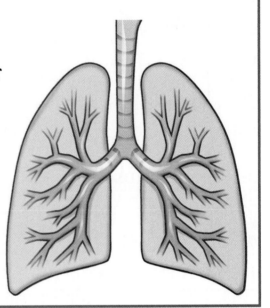

ACTIVITIES

1. Try to say something while you're breathing in. Try to say something while you're breathing out. Which is easier?

2. Breathe onto a mirror. What happens? Rinse your mouth with cold water. Again breathe on the mirror. What happens?

The Muscular System

The muscles in your body help you move. When you blink, you are using muscles. When you run, you are using muscles. Even when you eat, you are using muscles.

Caring for Your Muscular System

Stretch your muscles before you use them for play or exercise.

ACTIVITY

Wiggle your nose.
Stick out your tongue.
Wrinkle your forehead.
Smile. Are you using muscles?

face muscles

neck muscles

arm muscles

stomach muscles

leg muscles

The Nervous System

brain

nerves

Your nervous system makes your muscles work and tells you about your surroundings. Your brain and your nerves are parts of your nervous system.

Caring for Your Nervous System

Get plenty of sleep. Sleeping lets your brain rest.

ACTIVITY

Have a classmate blindfold you and fill one cup with cold water and another cup with warm water. Stick your finger in each cup. Can you tell which is the cold water and which is the warm water?

GLOSSARY

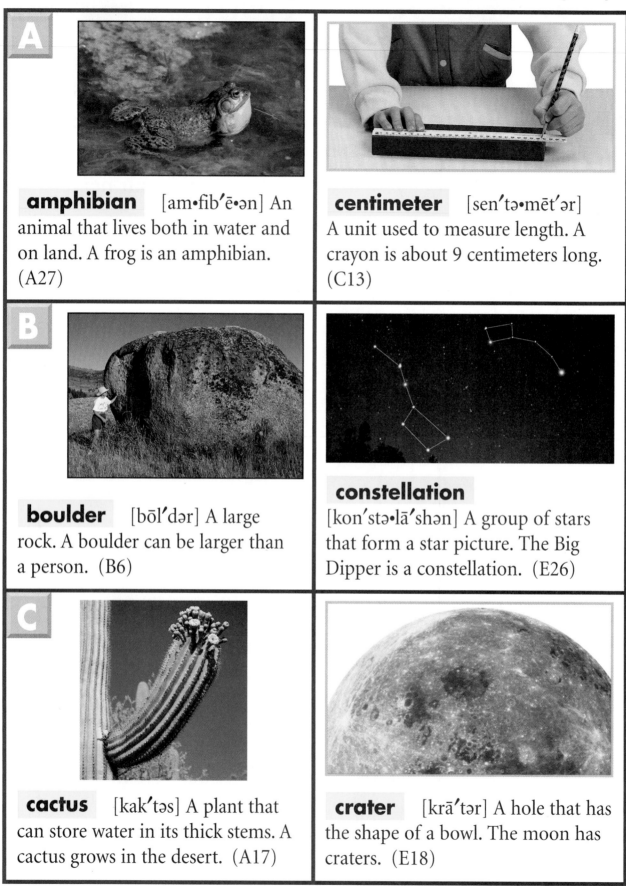

A

amphibian [am·fib′ē·ən] An animal that lives both in water and on land. A frog is an amphibian. (A27)

centimeter [sen′tə·mēt′ər] A unit used to measure length. A crayon is about 9 centimeters long. (C13)

B

boulder [bōl′dər] A large rock. A boulder can be larger than a person. (B6)

constellation [kon′stə·lā′shən] A group of stars that form a star picture. The Big Dipper is a constellation. (E26)

C

cactus [kak′təs] A plant that can store water in its thick stems. A cactus grows in the desert. (A17)

crater [krā′tər] A hole that has the shape of a bowl. The moon has craters. (E18)

D

digest [di•jest′] To break down food in the body. It is harder to digest an apple than apple juice. (A61)

E

energy [en′ər•jē] Something that can cause change and do work. Light and heat are kinds of energy. (E6)

dinosaur [dī′nə•sôr′] An animal that lived millions of years ago. Tyrannosaurus rex was a dinosaur. (B37)

extinct [ek•stingkt′] No longer living. Because dinosaurs do not live anymore, they are extinct. (B37)

drought [drout] A long time without rain. Many plants die during a drought. (E38)

F

force [fôrs] A push or a pull that makes something move. Magnetism is one kind of force. (C59)

fossil [fos′əl] What is left of a plant or an animal that lived long ago. A fossil can be a print of an animal's bones. (B27)

gravity [grav′i•tē] A force that pulls things toward the center of Earth. Earth's gravity is stronger than the moon's. (C63)

G

gas [gas] The only kind of matter that always fills all the space inside a container. Balloons are filled with a gas. (C21)

H

heart [härt] A muscle that pumps blood to every part of the body. Your heart is the size of your fist. (A55)

germinate [jûr′mə•nāt′] To start to grow. A seed may germinate if it gets water and warmth. (A10)

heart rate [härt′ rāt′] How fast or slowly a heart beats. Exercise makes the heart rate faster. (A56)

I

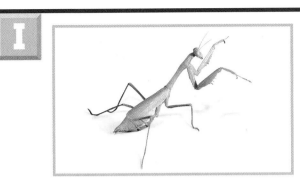

insect   [in'sekt'] An animal that has three body parts and six legs. Ants and bees are each a kind of insect. (A28)

liquid   [lik'wid] A form of matter that does not have its own shape. Water, milk, juice, and gasoline are each a liquid. (C15)

irreversible   [ir'ri·vûr'sə•bəl] Not able to be changed back. Cooking an egg causes an irreversible change. (C48)

litter   [lit'ər] Trash that is not put in a trash can. Plants and animals are hurt by litter. (E44)

L

life cycle   [lif' si'kəl] All the parts of an animal's life from birth to death. The life cycle of a bird has different stages. (A31)

living   [liv'ing] Growing and changing. Plants and animals are living things because they grow and change. (A5)

R29

location [lō•kā′shən] The place where something is. You can push or pull something to change its location. (C60)

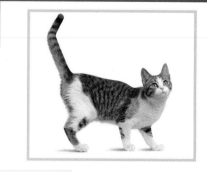

mammal [mam′əl] An animal that has fur or hair. A mother mammal makes milk to feed to her young. A cat is a mammal. (A26)

loudness [loud′nis] How loud or soft a sound is. A sound's loudness depends on the amount of energy used to make the sound. (C86)

mass [mas] The amount of matter an object has. You can use a balance to see how much mass an object has. (C7)

lungs [lungz] Body parts that help you breathe the air you need to live. When you breathe in, air moves into your lungs. (A55)

matter [mat′ər] What all things are made of. People, clothing, air, and water are all made of matter. (C5)

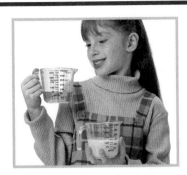

milliliter [mil′i•lēt′ər] A unit used to measure the volume of a liquid. Some measuring cups measure in milliliters. (C19)

moon [mo͞on] The largest object you can see in the night sky. The moon takes about one month to orbit Earth. (E17)

mineral [min′ər•əl] One kind of nonliving thing that is found in nature. Copper and iron are each a mineral. (B18)

moonlight [mo͞on′līt′] The light from the moon. Light from the sun that bounces off the moon is called moonlight. (E17)

mixture [miks′chər] Something made up of two or more things that do not change. Taco filling is a mixture. (C36)

motion [mō′shən] The act of moving. People, animals, and things are in motion when they move. (C67)

muscles [mus′əlz] Body parts that move your bones and do other jobs. Your muscles work in pairs. (A51)

nonliving [non•liv′ing] Not alive. Air, water, and rocks are nonliving things. (A5)

music [myo͞o′zik] A combination of sounds that people enjoy. You can use an instrument to make music. (C95)

nutrients [no͞o′trē•ənts] Minerals. Plants need nutrients from the soil to grow. (A9)

N

natural resource [nach′ər•əl rē′sôrs′] Something found in nature that people can use to meet their needs. Rocks are one natural resource. (B7)

O

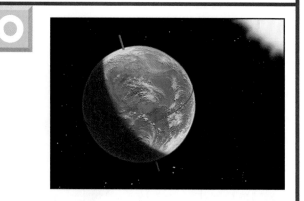

orbit [ôr′bit] The path around something. Earth's orbit around the sun takes one year. (E12)

P

paleontologist

[pā′lē•ən•tol′ə•jəst′] A scientist who finds and studies fossils. This paleontologist studies dinosaurs. (B29)

pollution [pə•loo′shən] Waste that harms land, water, or air. Some factories and cars can make pollution. (E43)

permanent teeth

[pûr′mə•nənt tēth′] Adult teeth that take the place of first teeth. People have 32 permanent teeth. (A46)

property [prop′ər•tē] A quality of something. Color, size, shape, and texture are each a property. (C7)

pitch [pich] How high or low a sound is. The pitch of a cat's meow is higher than the pitch of a lion's roar. (C87)

R

reconstruct [rē′kən•strukt′] To rebuild. Scientists reconstruct dinosaur skeletons. (B34)

recycle [rē•sĭ′kəl] To use old materials to make new things. You can recycle metal, plastic, and paper to make other things. (E51)

reuse [rē′yo͞oz′] To use again. You can reuse a water bottle as a flower vase. (E51)

reptile [rep′tīl] An animal that has rough, dry skin. Snakes and lizards are each a kind of reptile. (A27)

reversible [ri•vûr′sə•bəl] Able to be changed. The freezing of water is reversible. (C43)

resource [rē′sôrs′] Anything that people can use. People use resources for food and shelter. (B7)

rock [rok] A hard, nonliving thing that comes from the Earth. People use rocks to build roads and buildings. (B5)

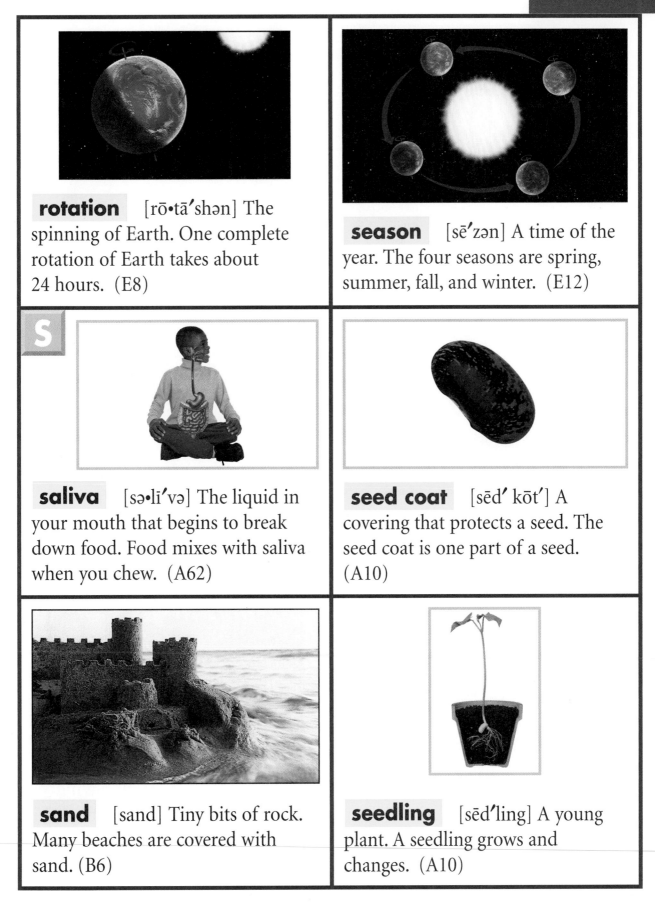

rotation [rō•tā′shən] The spinning of Earth. One complete rotation of Earth takes about 24 hours. (E8)

season [sē′zən] A time of the year. The four seasons are spring, summer, fall, and winter. (E12)

S

saliva [sə•lī′və] The liquid in your mouth that begins to break down food. Food mixes with saliva when you chew. (A62)

seed coat [sēd′ kōt′] A covering that protects a seed. The seed coat is one part of a seed. (A10)

sand [sand] Tiny bits of rock. Many beaches are covered with sand. (B6)

seedling [sēd′ling] A young plant. A seedling grows and changes. (A10)

R35

skeleton [skel′ə•tən] The bones that hold up the body and give it shape. (A50)

solid [sol′id] The only form of matter that has a shape of its own. Books, furniture, and cars are each a solid. (C9)

soil [soil] The loose top layer of Earth's surface. People use soil to grow food. (B5)

sonar [sō′när′] A way to use sounds to locate objects under water. Dolphins use a natural sonar by listening to echoes. (C92)

solar energy [sō′lər en′ər•jē] Light and heat from the sun. Living things on Earth are warmed by solar energy. (E7)

sound [sound] Energy that you hear. A sound can be loud or soft. (C79)

stomach [stum′ək] A body part made of muscles that squeeze food and mix it with special juices. (A63)

Triceratops [trī•ser′ə•tops′] A kind of dinosaur that had three horns on its head. Triceratops was a plant eater. (B38)

sun [sun] The star closest to Earth. The sun is much larger than it looks from Earth. (E6)

V

vibrate [vī′brāt′] To move back and forth very fast. The strings of a guitar vibrate when you pluck them. (C79)

T

transportation [trans′pər•tā′shən] Ways to move people or things. Ships, cars, and airplanes are kinds of transportation. (B13)

W

wind [wind] The force of moving air. Wind can move sailboats, kites, pinwheels, and wind vanes. (C62)

R37

P

Paleontologists, B29
and fossils, B33, B34, B35
learning about dinosaurs, B40–B41, B43
Paper, reuse, E54
People
and the environment, E49–E53
growth, A42, A43–A47, A71
using air, B15, B17
using minerals, B19
using natural resources, B15
using plants, B16–B17
using rock, B7
using soil, B5, B9
using sound, C95
using water, B10, B11–B13, B20
Percussion instruments, C96–C97, C98, C99
Permanent teeth, A46
Personal trainer, C73
Pets, A37
Pitch, C76, C87
Planets, E25

Plants
cactus, A17
cotton, B16
growth, A9–A11, A70, A71
kinds of, A15, A16–A17
and light, A13
natural resource, B15, B16–B17
needs, A8, A12–A13
parts, A9
pine tree, A16, B16
seeds, A9, A10, A16, A18, E36, E41
uses, B16–B17
Pollution, E43
air, E45
and environment, E43
land, E44
water, E46, E47
Property, of matter, C7
Pull, C58, C59, C60, C71
Push, C58, C59, C60–C61
and exercises, C73

R

Rain, C42
and habitats, E37–E39
Recycle, E51, E58

Reptiles, A27
alligator, A25
chameleon, A27
Resource, B7
Respiratory system, R22–R23
Reuse, E48, E51, E54, E58
Reversible, C43, C46
Rock, B5
fossils, B33
kinds of, B6
uses, B7
Roots, A9
Rotation, E8
on axis, E11
Ruler, A36, C29, R5

S

Safety
bike, R18–R19
fire, R16
stranger, R17
Sand, B2, B6
Sandstone, B6
Sandy soil, B8
Scelidosaurus, B42
School nurse, A67
Scientists
archaeologist, E55
naturalist, A19
paleontologist, B29
Scott, David, E19
Seasons, E11–E15
on calendar, E28

Trash
> and archaeologists, E55
> less, E51
> as litter, E44
> reuse, E54

Triceratops, B38–B39, B40

Tyrannosaurus rex, B38–B39, B40

V

Vibrate, C79
> in air, C80–C81, C82, C83
> for different sounds, C84, C85–C87, C88, C89–C93, C96, C98, C99
> in the eardrum, C82
> vocal cords, C83

Vibrations, C80–C81, C82–C83, C84, C85, C87, C88, C89–C93, C96, C98–C99

Vocal cords, C83

Volume, liquid, C19

W

Walnuts, A18

Waste, E43, E44, E46

Water
> changes, C38, C39–C43
> moving, C62
> plants need, A9, A12, A17
> in soil, B8
> solid, C40, C42
> uses, B10, B11–B13, B20

Water pollution, E42, E46
> and litter, E47
> preventing, E53

Water vapor, C39, C41–C42

Weather
> and habitats, E37–E41
> in seasons, E12–E13
> and seeds, E36

Weathering,
> **of rocks,** B46

Wind, C62

Wind instruments, C99

Wood, uses, B16

Photography Credits: Page placement key: (t) top, (c) center, (b) bottom, (l) left, (r) right, (bg) background, (i) inset

Cover: Robert Winslow

Unit A: A1 J. & W. Waldman/Bruce Coleman, Inc.; A1 (bg) Keith Lanpher/Liaison International; A2-A3 Ken Biggs/Tony Stone Images; A3 (i) Connie Hansen/The Stock Market; A6 (t) John D. Cunningham/Visuals Unlimited; A6 (b) Tim Davis/Photo Researchers; A12 Grant Heilman Photography, Inc.; A13 (t) Cathlyn Melloan/Tony Stone Images; A13 (b) David R. Frazier; A15 (t) David Lawrence/Panoramic Images; A15 (c) Gary Irving/Panoramic Images; A15 (b) Morey K. Milbradt/Panoramic Images; A16 (t) Doug Sokell/Tom Stack & Associates; A16 (ti) Dr. Wm. M. Harlow/Photo Researchers; A16 (c) Michael Groen Photography; A16 (b) Superstock; A16 (bi) Runk/Schoenberger/Grant Heilman Photography, Inc.; A17 (l) Gene Ahrens/Bruce Coleman, Inc.; A17 (r) Doug Sokell/Tom Stack & Associates; A17 (ti) Superstock; A18 (t) Danilo Donadoni/Bruce Coleman, Inc.; A18 (c) J. C. Carton/Bruce Coleman, Inc.; A18 (b) G. I. Bernard/Animals Animals/Earth Scenes; A20 (l) Jeff Foott/DRK Photo; A20 (c) John D. Cunningham/Visuals Unlimited; A20 (r) Wayne Lankinen/DRK Photo; A21 Michael Groen Photography; A22-A23 Flip Nicklin/Minden Pictures; A23 (i) Richard R. Hansen/Photo Researchers; A25 (t) S. J. Krasemann/Photo Researchers; A25 (c) Tom Zezo/The Wildlife Collection; A25 (bl) John E. Swedberg/Bruce Coleman, Inc.; A25 (bc) Mark Wagoner/Gamma-Liaison International; A25 (br) Peter Davey/Bruce Coleman, Inc.; A26 (t) G. Robert Bishop/Tony Stone Images; A26 (b) Wayne Lankinen/DRK Photo; A27 (t) Renee Lynn/Tony Stone Images; A27 (c) Michael Fogden/DRK Photo; A27 (b) Denise Tackett/Tom Stack & Associates; A28 (t) Marty Cordano/DRK Photo; A28 (b) J. Carmichael/Bruce Coleman, Inc.; A29 (l) Brian Parker/Tom Stack & Associates; A29 (r) Rex Ziak/Tony Stone Images; A31 (t) Mark Newman/Bruce Coleman, Inc.; A31 (b) S. J. Krasemann/Peter Arnold, Inc.; A32 (t) Tim Davis/Photo Researchers; A32 (b) William H. Mullins/Photo Researchers; A33 (t) Arthur C. Twomey/Photo Researchers; A33 (c) Michael Habicht/Animals Animals/Earth Scenes; A33 (b) Jennifer Loomis/Animals Animals/Earth Scenes; A34, A35 (l) Jane Burton/AG Stock USA; A36 David M. Dennis/Tom Stack & Associates; A37 (l) Renee Lynn/Tony Stone Images; A37 (c) Patricia Doyle/Tony Stone Images; A37 (r) Lemoine Jacana/Photo Researchers; A37 (ri) Breck P. Kent/Animals Animals/Earth Scenes; A38 Kathi Lamm/Tony Stone Images; A39 (l) Ed Reschke/Peter Arnold, Inc.; A39 lc Rod Planck/Photo Researchers; A39 (rc) Jeff Foott/DRK Photo; A39 (r) D. Cavagnaro/DRK Photo; A40-A41 Index Stock Photography; A43 (frames) Michael Groen Photography; A43 (l) Mary T. Murphy; A43 (r) Mary Kay Taylor; A44-A45 Stephen Ogilvy/Picture It; A46 Paul Avis/Gamma-Liaison International; A47 (t) Steve Dunwell/Image Bank; A49-A52 (l) Stephen Ogilvy/Picture It; A52-A53 David Madison/Bruce Coleman, Inc.; A53 (i) S. Villeger/Photo Researchers; A55-A57 Stephen Ogilvy/Picture It; A59 Tom & Dee Ann McCarthy/The Stock Market; A61-A63 Stephen Ogilvy/Picture It; A64 Richard Hutchings/Picture It; A66 Mehau Kulyk/SPL/Photo Researchers; A68 Stephen Ogilvy/Picture It.

Unit B: Pg. B1 Howard Grey/Tony Stone Images; B1 (bg) Alan Kearney/FPG International; B2-B3 David Ball/The Stock Market; B3 (i) Richard Megna/Fundamental Photographs; B5 Lee Foster/Bruce Coleman, Inc.; B6-B7 (t) Tom Bean/Tom Bean Photography; B6 (b), B7 (c) Michael Groen Photography; B7 (b) David Ball/The Stock Market; B7 (bi) N. P. Alexander/Visuals Unlimited; B8-B9 (t) Uniphoto; B9 (b) Bill Everitt/Tom Stack & Associates; B11 (t) Uniphoto; B11 (bl) Alese/Mort Pechter/The Stock Market; B11 (br), B12 (t) Stephen Ogilvy/Picture It; B12 (c) Tom & Dee Ann McCarthy/The Stock Market; B12 (b) David Madison/Tony Stone Images; B13 (t) Seth Goltzer/The Stock Market; B13 (b) Jeff Greenberg/PhotoEdit; B16 (t) Michael Lisnet/Gamma-Liaison International; B16 (b), B17 (ti), B17 (bi) Michael Groen Photography; B17 (t) Jonathan Rehg/Gamma-Liaison International; B17 (b) Stephen Ogilvy/Picture It; B18 (tl) Chris D. Winters/Photo Researchers; B18 (cl) Biophoto Associates; B18 (cr) Michael Groen Photography; B18 (bl) A. W. Ambler/Photo Researchers; B18 (br) Smith & Hawken; B19 Richard Hutchings/PhotoEdit; B20 (t) Lawrence Migdale/Stock, Boston; B20 (cl) Ed Malitsky/Gamma-Liaison International; B20 (c) Stephen Frisch/Stock, Boston; B20 (cr) David Madison/Tony Stone Images; B20 (b) Michael Groen Photography; B21 (t) Tomas Muscionico/Contact Press Images; B21 (b) Tim Thayer/Gagosian Gallery; B22 (cl) Tom Bean/Tom Bean Photography; B22 (cr) Debra Ferguson/AG Stock USA; B22 (bl) Michael Groen Photography; B22 (br) Dick Spahr/Gamma-Liaison International; B23 (t) Stephen Ogilvy/Picture It; B24-B25 Tom McHugh/Photo Researchers; B27, B28-B29 (t), John Cancalosi/Peter Arnold, Inc.; B29 (b) R. T. Nowitz/R. T. Nowitz Photos; B30 (t) David J. Sams/Tony Stone Images; B30 (c) David Schwimmer/Bruce Coleman, Inc.; B30 (b) Jon Cancalosi/Stock, Boston; B31 (t) E. R. Degginger/Bruce Coleman, Inc.; B31 (c) Earl Scott/Photo Researchers; B31 (b) Peter Menzel/Stock, Boston; B33 Les Stone/Sygma; B34 (l) David R. Frazier/Photo Researchers; b34 (r) Rich Frishman/Tony Stone Images; B35 (t) D. B. Dutheil/Sygma; B35 (b) Patrick Aventurier/Gamma-Liaison International; B37 Mark Perlstein/Black Star; B38-B39 (b) C. Chesek & D. Finnin/American Museum of Natural History; B39 (t) The Royal Tyrrell Museum Library; B40 Bruce Selyem Photo/Museum of the Rockies; B40 (bl) A. J. Copley/Visuals Unlimited; B41 (t) Francois Gohier/Photo Researchers; B41 (b) Linda J. Moore; B43 (t) Louis Psihoyos/Matrix; B43 (b) Stephen Ogilvy/Picture It; B44 Louis Psihoyos/Matrix; B45 David M. Dennis/Tom Stack & Associates.

Unit C: Pg. C1 Into The Wind; C1 (bg) Simon Fraser/SPL/Photo Researchers; C2-C3 G. Brad Lewis/Gamma-Liaison International; C5, C6 (tl), C7 Stephen Ogilvy/Picture It; C6 (tr), C6 (b) Michael Groen Photography; C9 Richard Hutchings/Picture It; C10, C11 Michael Groen Photography; C12, C13 (r) Stephen Ogilvy/Picture It; C16, C17 Michael Groen Photography; C18, C19 Stephen Ogilvy, Picture It: C21 Joseph Sohm/The Stock Market; C22 (l) Pat Lanza/Bruce Coleman, Inc.; C22 (r) Stephen Ogilvy/Picture It; C23 (t) Royce Bair/Uniphoto; C23 (c), C23 (b) Richard Hutchings/Picture It; C24-C25 Stephen Ogilvy/Picture It; C25 (t) U.S. Dept. of Transportation; C25 (b), C27 (t), C28 (l), C28 (c) Michael Groen Photography; C28 (r), C29 Stephen Ogilvy/Picture It; C30-C31 Scott T. Smith/The Stock Solution; C31 (i) Arlene L. Parnes/Photo Researchers; C32 Bryan F. Peterson/The Stock Market; C33, C34-C35, C36, C37 Michael Groen Photography; C39 Giovanni Simeone/The Stock Market; C42 Bob Lewellyn/Uniphoto; C42 (i) S. Dooley/Gamma-Liaison International; C43 (t) W. A. Banaszewski/Visuals Unlimited; C43 (b) Michael Deyoung/Uniphoto; C45, C46 (b) Michael Groen Photography; C46 (t), C47 Stephen Ogilvy/Picture It; C48 Barbara Leslie/FPG International; C49 Michael Groen Photography; C51 (t) Martha Cooper/Peter Arnold, Inc.; C52 (tl) Michael Groen Photography; C52 (tc) Aaron Haupt/Stock, Boston; C52 (tr) Barbara Leslie/FPG International; C52 (bc) George Mattei/Envision; C52 (b) Michael Groen Photography; C56-C57 Laguna Photo/Gamma-Liaison International; C57 (i) Brian Parker/Tom Stack & Associates; C60 (t) David R. Frazier/Photo Researchers; C60 (bl), C61 (t) Stephen Ogilvy/Picture It; C62 (t) Don Kreuter/Rainbow; C62 (b) Richard Pasley/Stock, Boston; C63 (t) MacDonald Photography/Unicorn Stock Photos; C63 (b) Stephen Ogilvy/Picture It; C67 Frank Pennington/Unicorn Stock Photos; C68 (tr) Richard Pasley/Stock, Boston; C68-C69 (b) Richard Hutchings/Picture It; C70 (b) Jim Cummins/FPG International; C74 (tl) B. Daemmrich/Image Works; C74 (tlc) Jim Cummins/FPG International; C74 (tc) Richard Hutchings/Picture It; C74 (tr) Frank Pennington/Unicorn Stock Photos; C74 (b) MacDonald Photography/Unicorn Stock Photos; C76-C77 Tim Davis/Tony Stone Images; C77 (i) Robert P. Carr/Bruce Coleman, Inc.; C79 A. Ramey/PhotoEdit; C80 (r) Richard Hutchings/PhotoEdit; C81 (t) Michael Groen Photography; C81 (b) Spencer Grant/PhotoEdit; C82, C83 (l) Stephen Ogilvy/Picture It; C85 Ken Graham/Bruce Coleman, Inc.; C86 Stephen Ogilvy/Picture It; C87 (t) Barbara Gerlach/DRK Photo; C87 (b) Stephen J. Krasemann/DRK Photo; C89 Stacy Pick/Stock Boston; C90 (t) Stephen Ogilvy/Picture It; C92 Stuart Westmorland/Tony Stone Images; C92-C93 Amos Nachoum/The Stock Market; C95 Eric Freedman/Bruce Coleman, Inc.; C99 (tcl) Spencer Grant/PhotoEdit; C99 (tr) Doug Martin/Photo Researchers; C100 (#2) A. Ramey/PhotoEdit; C100 (#3l) Renee Lynn/Photo Researchers; C100 (#3r) Robert Haddock/Tony Stone Images; C100 (a) Stephen J. Krasemann/DRK Photo; C100 (b) Stuart Westmorland/Tony Stone Images.